AT LONG LAST LOVE

AT LONG LAST LOVE

SAGE ADVICE AND
TRUE STORIES FROM
AMERICA'S PREMIER
MATCHMAKERS

John Wingo, Ph.D., and Julie Wingo, M.A.

WARNER BOOKS

A Time Warner Company

Warner Books, Inc., 1271 Avenue of the Americas, New York, NY 10020

A Time Warner Company

Printed in the United States of America

First Printing: April 1994

10 9 8 7 6 5 4 3 2 1

Library of Congress Cataloging-in-Publication Data

Wingo, John.
    At long last love : sage advice and true stories from America's premier
matchmakers / John Wingo, and Julie Wingo.
        p. cm.
    ISBN 0-446-51729-1
    1. Man-woman relationships. 2. Love. I. Wingo, Julie.
    II. Title.
HQ801.W74 1994
306.7—dc20   93-21892
                                                                    CIP

To Keirsten and Jessica
for proving that the institution
of marriage is alive and well.

Acknowledgments

We wish to thank D. Patrick Miller for refining our perceptions, asking the right questions and often providing many of the "answers." There would be no book without his gentle ability to listen and craft something meaningful from our scattered babblings. He is, quite simply, one of the most complete writers on the planet.

We wish also to thank Linda Chester and Laurie Fox for their understanding during the manuscript submission and writing phases of the book. Their professionalism and upbeat personalities always shielded us from chaos and despair.

Many of our clients provided feedback to a myriad of questions about the journey to find a meaningful relationship. Their excitement and belief in us kept us going.

We owe everyone at Warner Books our gratitude. It is impossible to imagine a more supportive group of professionals. Special thanks to Fredda Isaacson for giving us the chance and to Susan Suffes, our kind and talented editor, for making it go so smoothly.

Contents

CHAPTER 1   1

At Long Last Love:
Is Romance Still Possible?
> Who Are We?; Why Is It So Tough to Meet
> Someone?; Do You Really Want a Relationship?;
> Why Look for Love?; How We Met

CHAPTER 2   17

Facing the Odds:
What Are the Real Problems in Today's
Search for Love?
> **Andrea's Story;** Staying Out of Trouble; Voices
> from the Search; Fast Women, Fast Men Too; Look-
> ing for Mr. Goodlooks; The Inner Barriers; Twenty
> Common Attitudes: Are You Getting in Your Own
> Way? Our Secret

CHAPTER 3   49

Who Are You?
What Do You Want? And What Do You Really Need?
> **Louise's Story;** Facing the Facts; How Much
> Self-Knowledge Do You Need?; How Realistic Are
> You About Yourself?; Self-Assessment Factors;
> What Do You Really Need in a Mate?; Desire
> Assessment Factors; Are You Changing?

CHAPTER 4   87

Learning from Your Past:
What Have You Been Doing Wrong—and Right?
> **Greg's Story;** Recognizing Unproductive Patterns;

Changing Unproductive Patterns; What Have You
Been Doing Right?; Looking Back: Questions for
Reflection; Leaving an Unhealthy Relationship;
Five Rules for Leaving

CHAPTER 5   113
Across a Crowded Room:
Encounters of the First Kind
William's Story; Is There a Right Way?; Review-
ing the Ways to Meet People: *Print Personals, Tele-
phone Matching, Video Dating, Private Networking,
Singles Clubs, Singles Bars and Parties, Professional Or-
ganizations, Sports, Hobby, and Special-Interest Groups,
Professional Matchmakers*; Arranging First Encoun-
ters; First-Date Assessment: How Did It Go?

CHAPTER 6   147
From Dating to Relating:
Encounters of the Continuing Kind
Hilary's Story; Signals for Singles; Old-Fashioned
Flirting; Four Check-offs for a Developing
Relationship; The Wingo 51-80 Principle;
Applying the 51-80 Principle; Sexual Timing;
Developing Sexual Discretion; Sexual Etiquette;
Warning Signs of Unhealthy Relating

CHAPTER 7   187
Deciding for Devotion:
How to Approach the Issues of Commitment
May's Story; Taking the Big Step; The Major Issues
of Commitment; What Kind of Commitment? And
When?; Four Guidelines for Improving
Communication Skills; Preparing for the Stages of
Life Together

APPENDIX   215
Special Messages for Women and for Men

AT
LONG
LAST
LOVE

1

At Long Last Love: Is Romance Still Possible?

Love will find a way.

—popular proverb

If you've picked up this book for personal reasons, your love life is probably not what you'd like it to be. Are you feeling that the last relationship you had is just that—the last one? Are you still getting over a hurtful breakup, perhaps from a serious, long-term relationship or marriage? Or are you tired of a series of short, unfulfilling involvements? Are you pleased with your professional achievements and career position, yet feel that the demands of your work are keeping you from meeting your lifemate? Are you in your fifties or sixties, and worried that it's just too late to find a new life partner? Or have you been burned so many times in love that you've just given up the search?

If any of these questions apply to you, take heart—this book is intended to give you a new way of looking at these and many other modern problems of romance and relation-

1

ship. Having advised and arranged meetings for thousands of people over the last nine years, we know just how tough it is to find someone to love and share your life with. But we also know that it's possible, and worth far more than all the effort that's required and all the disappointment you may experience along the way.

WHO ARE WE?

There's a good chance that this isn't the first "singles" book you've looked over. There are some good ones and some not-so-good ones on the market, and sometimes they're a little difficult to tell apart. What's different about this one? So far as we know, *this is the first book by a married couple with years of experience running a professional matchmaking service*. Our company is J. Wingo International (JWI), founded in 1985 and based in San Francisco. We have arranged quality introductions for thousands of people in this country and around the world. JWI caters to a successful and accomplished clientele who find out about us through our advertising or word-of-mouth recommendations.

Every month we arrange more than a hundred meetings between people who we think may be compatible, and we frequently talk to our clients by phone to help them sort through questions and communication difficulties that have cropped up in their dating experience. We've heard thousands of dating stories from our clients since we got started, and from them we have filtered out what we think is the best practical wisdom on how to meet people, how to arrange first dates, and how to turn exciting first dates into second and third ones.

There are several things that we are not that you should know about. First, we're not psychologists or marriage counselors. Our professional backgrounds are in communication and education, and as a result we've developed a pragmatic philosophy that emphasizes both endeavors. We believe that the search for a lifelong lover must be a journey of self-discovery that helps you become a more open, communicative, and honest person along the way. Many people involved in our program report that they've learned a lot more about themselves than they ever expected, as they grow better at evaluating themselves and their real needs. We count that as a kind of success that's just as important as the romances, committed relationships, and marriages that our service generates.

Second, we're not ivory-tower experts with a pet theory that promises a perfectly efficient or effortless approach to love. There's no foolproof method, special technique, or secret lingo to be found in this book. Instead, we're offering the sum of our experience and observations so far in the matchmaking business. We have the advantage of having talked to thousands of people on searches similar to yours, but of course no one but you knows exactly what your life is like. We like to think that we help people stay in touch with their own common sense about an aspect of life that many people are not very sensible about—but you still have to decide when we're making sense for *you* and when we're not.

Finally, we don't pretend to have the ideal relationship that all our clients should emulate. We do have two decades of marriage and a good family life to our credit, and that's no mean accomplishment in these chaotic times. But it hasn't all been smooth sailing for us—especially not the earliest years of our relationship. Later we'll share the story of our own match so that you can see we've experienced some of the typical mistakes, false starts, and heartbreaks that all human beings seem to experience.

WHY IS IT SO TOUGH TO MEET SOMEONE?

How often we've heard this complaint from frustrated singles: "There's just nobody interesting out there!" How rarely do we hear people admit, "Maybe I'm doing something wrong—or not doing everything I could." Believe it or not, we just don't think there's a nebulous dark cloud that hovers over unlucky singles, blocking them from ever finding someone to love. We do think that a lot of people engage in self-defeating behaviors, or only half-heartedly try out the various avenues for meeting people. "Well, I read the personals," a man says plaintively. Yes, but has he ever placed or responded to one? "I joined a singles club!" protests a woman—but has she attended more than one meeting? "Yes, I've tried networking," claims another—but it turns out that she's only asked her best girlfriend about her cute cousin, who turned out to be engaged.

Although the burgeoning singles market is sure to inspire more techniques and technologies to facilitate relationship matches, we don't think the solution for most people's frustrated searches lies in more or better high-tech. Rather, the solution is to be found in closer questioning of one's own intentions and motivations. This is the first step toward looking at the search for love in a new way.

Above all, the frustrated single person must consider this question: *Am I fully committed to the process of finding a mate, or am I emotionally ambivalent?* We see many people whose lonesomeness drives them into the search for a mate, a search that is then blocked every step of the way by their own resentment toward the other gender, bitterness about their past, or fearfulness about what an intimate partner might require of them. It's our opinion that anyone who's really ready to *find* love is ready to *give* it wholeheartedly. Then this equation comes into play:

$$\text{Enthusiasm} = \text{Magnetism} = \text{Luck}$$

So when it seems that your luck is down, it's time to assess your enthusiasm. It's the root energy that actually creates opportunities in the search for love.

Another important question: *Do I want a committed relationship enough to evaluate my lifestyle choices, and make changes if necessary?* We once heard a man complain about the way his lover was "clinging" to him and demanding more time together than he had to give her. Upon questioning, it turned out that after a year-long relationship, he was limiting their times together to Monday, Thursday, and Friday nights. "I work six and sometimes seven days a week," he said. "It's a very demanding schedule, so I like to have four nights a week when I can come home, relax, turn on the sports channel, and not have to answer to anybody."

We've heard similar reports from busy singles with established lifestyles who say that finding a mate is their number-one priority in life. Yet after three or four dates with someone they like, they may balk when the new relationship seems to threaten their habitual schedule or favorite ways of doing things. We're not saying that one must be ready to give up everything for romance. But flexibility

5

and an openness to change are key qualities for making the transition from merely dating someone to building a life together. Maybe you can work it out to have the couch, the popcorn, *and* a romantic partner on Friday nights—but you have to be willing to let the couch and the popcorn go! If you're not, you may be going at the search for love with ambivalent intentions, and that's an excellent way to stymie your quest.

DO YOU REALLY WANT A RELATIONSHIP?

Additionally, singles in their forties and older should consider this question: *Am I unconsciously building a single lifestyle to carry me for the rest of my life?* It's our observation that some people over thirty-five who have been single for six or seven years may be building secure and inflexible lifestyles because they're well on the way to preparing themselves to live alone for the rest of their lives. And that may be perfectly all right! Times are always changing, and our ideas of family and community are changing faster than ever before. In the near future, we're likely to see groups of older singles living in loose-knit but supportive communities that allow them a sense of family and connectedness without being mated to anyone over the long term. We're convinced that some people just don't need intimate bonding as much as others and can live quite well on their own. Needy people who are desperate for a relationship—and therefore quite likely to bond—may not be as psychologically healthy as some independent single people.

The salient question is whether one is *aware* of making the choice to live alone for the long term. We can tell that the process of deciding is already underway when new clients tell us that they're considering our service as a "last shot" at finding a committed relationship. Implicit in that kind of message is usually another one: "I'm not likely to change very much for the sake of a relationship. A mate will have to fit pretty well into my life the way it is." Put two people like this together, of course, and their long-term bonding potential goes way down.

Even if one person is willing to fit into another's fixed lifestyle, there will often be some kind of emotional imbalance that's not healthy or sustainable. Young people of either sex may marry older partners for their money or parental influence; a very insecure person may marry someone who tells him or her what to do about everything. These kinds of relationships may serve one or both partners' short-term purposes, but they tend to be unstable or even destructive in the long run.

Anyone of any age who is repeatedly failing to make connections in the search for love must consider these choices:

Is it more important (a) to fulfill every facet of the life you've already planned, or (b) to have a relationship?

Is it more important (a) to do all the things you want to do when you want to do them, or (b) to have a relationship?

Is it more important (a) to keep your life safe, predictable, and routine, or (b) to have a relationship?

Is it more important (a) not to have to explain or be

responsible to anyone for your behavior, or (b) to have a relationship?

If you honestly lean toward the (a) answers more frequently than (b), then you'll simply be getting in your own way when you write a personal, network, record a video, join a singles club, or hire a matchmaker to help you find a mate. There's nothing more important than getting clear within yourself about what your real priorities and intentions are. If you finally decide that you want to find love because you have a lot that you want to share, then the existing ways to meet people (surveyed in detail in Chapter 5) will provide more than enough opportunities and excitement for you.

WHY LOOK FOR LOVE?

The desire for romance and intimacy is so universal that it may seem silly to ask why we look for love. Yet it's our observation that many people are searching "on automatic" for a mate, and haven't recently thought about what they're looking for in a positive way. In fact, they may be thinking chiefly about what they *don't* want—they don't want to be alone, they don't want to stay in an unhappy relationship, and so on. Most of this book is concerned with troubleshooting the problems of finding a mate, so let's put the difficulties aside for a few moments and review the rewards that make the search for love worthwhile.

● *Romance is wonderful.* There's nothing like falling in love—making that magical connection with someone and entering an "altered state" fueled only by your actual excitement and desire to be with each other. The world seems new when we fall in love because we let down some of our guard and let out parts of ourselves that are normally kept from view. But romance is not just an ecstatic experience in itself. Ideally, it helps you cement a bond of affection and caring that will last you through the more challenging stages of relationship to follow.

● *There's more to love than romance.* It's true that the "high" of romance doesn't last—at least, not at 100 percent of its original intensity. But what some people regard as a tragedy can be looked upon as an opportunity—because it's *after* romance that two people really start learning how to help and support each other. The key is to start building communication skills (see Chapter 7) as soon as you encounter the more challenging moments of relationship that are sure to follow the high of romance.

● *Being in love means becoming someone new.* Committing to love for the long term means that you will become someone you couldn't have become on your own—like a mother or father, for instance. But even if you don't start a family together, a long-term relationship offers both people the opportunity to deepen themselves and develop capacities they wouldn't have the chance to develop on their own. In fact, we often subconsciously choose our life partners for what they have to teach us. And sometimes what they have to teach us is what we've been unable or unwilling to learn until we've met just the right teacher. That's the real meaning of the challenge to "honor and obey" found within traditional wedding vows: not to do whatever our spouse tells us to do without questioning, but to recognize what our spouse has to teach us and respectfully accept his or her lessons.

Whenever you start feeling embittered or doubtful about your own search for love, it will help you to remember some of your peak moments of romance and relating. You might also want to write down what you're looking for in purely positive terms. You could even try your hand at your own "love story," casting yourself and your idea of a perfect lover in a fable about meeting, falling in love, overcoming some great obstacle together, and living happily ever after. Such a story might tell you some surprising things about yourself and your desires, and help you clarify exactly what you hope to find in an intimate companion.

HOW WE MET

Now for our own love story—the true tale of how John and Julie Wingo met, fell in love, fell apart, and put ourselves together again for good. The end of this love story is not written yet because we're still living it, finding out every day what it means to live happily ever after. Mind you, happiness is not the same as perfection, total gratification, or complete, unending harmony. For us, happiness is knowing that we both made the best possible choice for a partnership worth working hard on for the rest of our lives. Our shared career as matchmakers blossomed from our love story. We reflect on it often when trying to help people see what they really want in a lifemate, and how to correct the mistakes they may have made in their search so far.

We met as twenty-year-olds in a sociology seminar at Eastern Michigan University. In the midst of 300 people sitting in a large lecture hall, John spied a blonde head a few rows ahead of him that kept drawing his attention. Our relationship began in earnest a few days later when we found ourselves in the same study group, and soon we began dating.

JULIE: I remember being in a study group with John. My roommate and I were laughing and having a grand time, and here was this guy who kept wanting us to focus and get down to the task at hand. When John asked me out, I was impressed that he didn't just invite me down to the beer hall like most of the guys would. Instead he dressed in a suit and we went to see a live performance of *Pal Joey* in Ann Arbor. There was something so refreshing and stimulating about that, and I thought I was in college to learn and be stimulated in that way. So John really impressed me right away.

On our second date we were at a boring party when John told me he loved me, and I thought, "Oh, really?" It scared me—how could he possibly love me by the second date? Then I just wanted to go home.

John has always been more impetuous than I. I grew up in a modest, hardworking family environment in a Detroit suburb. I was raised Catholic with strong family values, and I had the expectation that I would get married and raise a family, although I wanted to travel for a while as a young woman. But I did everything the way you were supposed to. In college I was responsible, I didn't drink a lot or go to all-night parties. What amazed me about John was how bright he was, and how much he could get away with. When he was going out to drink beer with his friends I had to be studying hard, yet he always pulled everything off. He's the type who could make a U-turn right in front of the police and not get caught, but I'd get a ticket if my front bumper was hanging over the crosswalk.

Anyway, we didn't really date much in the year and a half we were both at Eastern Michigan, maybe eight or ten times. We just seemed to be pals, and John never lacked for female company. When we graduated I took a teaching job in Michigan, and John went on to graduate school for his masters, and later went to California for his Ph.D. I could tell when he was in between girlfriends because I'd get letters every now and then asking why I didn't go to graduate school and get on with my life. But I didn't like school. I was happy teaching and having a steady income, even though it wasn't much. The money enabled me to go skiing, which I've always loved, even back then when it wasn't so fashionable. I didn't buy fancy ski suits; I wore my brother's old winter clothes.

John transferred to Carbondale, Illinois, to finish his doctoral degree, and we started seeing each other again. Something seemed to be rekindled between us, and I remember that we made an agreement to get married when his doctoral thesis was accepted. John doesn't recall that; he has an interesting memory! Anyway, I was under the impression we would be married that fall, and then he changed his mind. I guess we didn't communicate very clearly to each other at that age; sometimes you hear only what you want to hear if you don't make sure of things between you. So John called off the wedding in August, and that was that. It was very painful for me; this was my first serious love.

A year and a half later I got a Christmas card from John's parents, telling me that he'd finally received his Ph.D. and had married. I thought "Good for him" and really wished him the best in my heart. In 1970, I moved to San Francisco on my own.

JOHN: I confess to being pretty immature when I was a young man doing a lot of dating. There wasn't an iota of teaching in my upbringing about delving into my own feelings, that I should ever talk about them or understand them. So I just plunged ahead with whatever I felt at the time, whether I was feeling insecure or in love. For instance, when I started college at the University of Michigan I spent my time drinking beer and trying to date as many girls as I could. I left after a year and a half before they could kick me out, and decided to go down south to a small school called Murray State College in Kentucky. My father had graduated from there and I figured it might provide me with a fresh academic start. I drove down on the day after Christmas in a 1953 Mercury with no windshield wipers or heater. I had to get through 500 miles of snowstorm, often looking out of the side window to see ahead. It was a little impulsive, but I made it!

The move was good for me. I became more serious about academics and decided that I wanted to be a college professor more than anything. I guess I wanted to wear corduroy coats with leather elbow patches and smoke a pipe. When I transferred to Eastern Michigan, my third school in three years, I walked into my first class and immediately noticed Julie sitting three or four rows ahead of me. I liked her from the start, but I did play the field in those days. We were never formally engaged, although we did discuss marriage.

But I transferred to yet another school after a year and a half, and we drifted apart. Two graduate schools later and

13

hundreds of miles away from Julie, I started dating a girl in Illinois. This relationship had more to do with being comfortable together than truly in love. But once we started living together, marriage seemed to be the next natural step. We were married in 1968, the day after I received my doctorate in Communications from Southern Illinois University. But I knew walking down the aisle with my first wife that something was wrong; it just didn't feel right. I think she knew this too. We tried hard for two and a half years, living in Mississippi where we both were on the faculty of Ole Miss.

When we separated I tried to call Julie the next day, but I couldn't find her new phone number and called her mother, who had orders from Julie not to tell me anything if I ever called. She wanted me and our memories to remain behind her, but I knew quite clearly by now that Julie was the right woman for me. Luckily for me, Julie's mom disobeyed her and told me Julie had moved to San Francisco, and gave me her number. When Julie would not return my calls, I got on a plane to the West Coast immediately, hoping I could persuade her to see me.

After shunning me for days, she finally agreed to meet. The sparks were there again for both of us, and I was happier than I could remember ever being before. We started dating again long-distance after that, as I was still teaching in Mississippi. I proposed to Julie six months later, and we married in San Francisco in August 1971.

I don't shirk responsibility for breaking off our relationship the first time. It took me a long time, and the experience of an unsuccessful marriage, to realize that what I had with Julie was just about as good as it gets in this world. Of course she had a terrific struggle with trusting me when we got together again; it could hardly be otherwise. I guess I was just lucky that she didn't throw me in the San Francisco Bay! But by the time we were finally together, our experience made me want to work harder on our marriage than I'd ever worked on anything. Twenty-two years and two beautiful daughters later, I guess you could say we pulled it off.

The story of our own match is a classic illustration of Shakespeare's warning that "the course of true love never did run smooth." Lots of single people nowadays could vouch for the truth of that, but we're concerned that many people are becoming so confused and embittered by their experiences that they're getting in the way of their own search for the lifelong love they deserve. Can anyone reasonably expect to find a mate to live and learn with in these tumultuous times? Or might it be better to batten down the hatches and try to ride out the storm alone?

All we can say is that we're in a marriage that gets a little better every single day, so we know it can be done. We're offering this book with the realization that finding true love is perhaps a little harder than ever before, but not impossible. You *can* make your way through all the thickets and swamps of dating in the '90s to find a lasting love—if you have a clear picture of the obstacles in your way and an honest idea of who you are and what you really need. That's what we're here to help you figure out.

2

Facing the Odds:
What Are the Real Problems
in Today's Search for Love?

*I am so convinced that love is a nuisance,
that I am delighted my friends and I are exempt.*
— Madame de La Fayette

*In a world where many people struggle to look and act like
anyone but themselves, forty-two-year-old Andrea was a
study in matchless presence. Striding confidently into our San
Francisco office dressed simply in a black linen pantsuit with
a cream silk blouse, she obviously knew how to present her
tall, thin frame to its best advantage. Her manner in greeting
us was businesslike but sincere, and within a few minutes of
sitting down to talk we were both impressed by her wit and
bracing honesty. With shoulder-length black hair framing
her lean, angular face and piercing gray-green eyes, Andrea
exhibited a beauty of power rather than delicacy. Some men
might have found her intimidating, but at first it was hard
to see why she would not have more than enough attention
from males of her age and social environment.*

As a West Coast editor for a major women's magazine,

*Andrea voiced many of the common complaints we often hear from busy and successful single people. "I'm holed up in the office all day—and glued to the phone," she said with a slight, tense smile. "About the only time I get to review articles is at night, so I take a lot of work home with me. It doesn't drive me **too** crazy—in fact, I mostly enjoy what I do and I'm not the nightlife type anyway." Gazing out the window, Andrea pointed at the busy street scene below and exclaimed, "Just find me a nice, quiet nerd down there somewhere who's looking for a permanent relationship." Abruptly shifting her gaze back to us, she added in a mock-serious tone, "A nerd with some substantial experience in back rubs, of course. That's about the only requirement I have left. A girl can't be too demanding these days, it seems."*

We all laughed, but Andrea's humor was clearly spiked with resentment. For the first time we noticed a wearied and defensive look in her eyes—a look that would become more frequent and intense as she revealed her emotional history with men. After getting the basic biography we needed, we asked Andrea why she had come to a professional matchmaker. Her tone grew quiet and a little bitter.

*"Well, my last relationship broke up about a year ago, and I guess I've just started coming out of the cocoon I went into afterward. But I'm getting too old for the dating scene. And I don't have evenings to waste meeting somebody's cousin—who usually turns out to be a functional illiterate, of course. I'm **not** going to put up with being grabbed at, and I am **not** going to write a personal ad, for God's sake. I'm here to cut my losses, you might say, and start off with better prospects. That's what you're here for, right?"*

John smiled and said, "We do our best." Julie nodded and then asked Andrea, "Can you tell us about that last boyfriend, if you don't mind? It helps us to know what kind of men you've been attracted to in the past."

Andrea tried to be flippant. "Oh well, that's easy enough. All losers. You know the type." John raised his eyebrows and Andrea's spiteful smile vanished. "Okay," she sighed. "I'll tell you about Tom. He was a real scoundrel."

As we found out over the next half hour, Tom the scoundrel was a corporate attorney with work habits similar to Andrea's, which meant that their two-year relationship consisted largely of weekend dates at nice restaurants, interspersed with sleep-overs at each other's apartment once or twice on weeknights. Andrea had fond memories of one five-day vacation she had taken with Tom, but otherwise her stories about him were so negative that we wondered what had held the relationship together as long as it lasted.

"I take my job seriously," Andrea remarked at one point, "but Tom was a complete workaholic. Every time I tried to talk about us he moved the conversation around to talk about how busy he was and how he couldn't see beyond the next year with the firm, and blah blah and so on. He just didn't have a world outside that job—until he told me about that cute young secretary that he had started seeing occasionally 'as a friend' and all that. I said, 'I get the message, buster. No need to say anything else. I'm out of here.'" Andrea paused as her eyes became moist, but then her voice hardened. "For a while I thought he just needed time, that he wasn't quite ready to commit. Then he had to prove that he was a total jerk, like all the rest of them."

19

So far, Andrea was telling us a story that was not uncommon but that was dramatically one-sided in the telling. After a few moments of silence in the room, Julie spoke up softly to say, "I can understand why this was so painful for you, Andrea. What I don't understand is what kept you two together for so long. Would you mind telling us what you liked about Tom? What do you remember as his good points?"

Andrea blinked and her eyes widened like a schoolgirl who wasn't prepared for a pop quiz. "His good points?" she murmured softly before letting her gaze drift up toward the ceiling, as if she were searching her mind for some long-forgotten address or phone number. A half minute passed in silence before Andrea spoke again, her voice a little uncertain for the first time since the conversation began.

"Well, I guess this is obvious, but Tom was very successful in his career. He could focus on a topic and explore it thoroughly." Andrea gave Julie a helpless look, as if she hoped this phase of the questioning might be over. But we both felt that Andrea needed a harder push, a challenge to her habitual way of looking at her relationships. "What else?" Julie pressed. "What did you first like about Tom personally?"

Andrea looked down at her fingernails for another ten seconds or so before reluctantly yielding a little more information. "He did make me laugh most of the time," she admitted. "I get a little down on the world sometimes, and he seemed to see something funny in almost everything. He was one of those people who can actually make up jokes, you know? I used to tell him he could be a great stand-up comic, but he said he didn't care for an audience of more than two or three—and that one was just perfect."

Andrea chuckled and her face seemed to soften. With a little more coaching, she was soon revealing to us that Tom actually had quite a bit going for him. "Tom was a man who made me think," Andrea said at one point. "He probably would have been a good father. . . . " As she talked on, it gradually became clear that their relationship had broken up not because Tom was a bad guy, but because both of them feared what commitment would mean to their careers and lifestyles. They simple did not know how to discuss their future in a careful, respectful way. Tom used his devotion to his career as an obstacle to intimacy, and Andrea probably overreacted to his first few defensive maneuvers—setting up a pattern of poor communication that only got worse as time went on. Up to this point, Andrea had also avoided taking any responsibility for this and her other relationship failures, leading her to become aloof and defensive.

Once this picture became clear to us, we had to be frank with Andrea about the invisible barriers to intimacy she was putting up. She had no idea that she was likely to be perceived by most of the men she met as embittered and unapproachable. "You're smart, attractive, and articulate," John told her. "We'll have no problem matching you with guys who will be delighted to spend some time with you. But let me level with you about something very important. It's my guess that you're likely to be pretty tough on the men you meet—just like you were pretty tough on Tom when you first told us about him. It took a while to find out what you liked about the guy. It's like pulling teeth to get you to say anything positive *about the men you've known. Are you aware of the problem that poses for us in trying to help you?"*

Andrea nodded slowly, her posture rigid. She was starting to get our message, but apparently she didn't like it so far. She hadn't expected us to be anything but supportive—after all, she was going to pay us!

"So," John continued, "it's going to be real important that you give the guys you meet a fair chance. I think you're pretty angry about what's happened in the past, but you'll have to find a way not to be so defensive on a first date. Maybe you should take another look at your relationship with Tom, and see if you can assess what went wrong without blaming either one of you. It sounds to me like Tom had his good points and his bad points, just like you and everybody else, but you're only remembering the downside. Believe me, that's going to affect the way you see all the men you meet. If you can't find a way to be fair, open-hearted, and approachable, paying us to find prospects for you won't be any help at all."

Obviously disconcerted, Andrea looked a little vulnerable for the first time since she had walked in the door. Her eyes went to the window, then across the room to a painting on the wall, and finally settled on Julie. It would take a couple minutes before she could look directly at John again. Finally she replied quietly, "I guess I'm a little embarrassed. I don't feel like such a hard person inside, but you may be right about how I look at men these days, and what they must think about me. I guess I expected you to believe everything I said and find somebody for me who would make me forget what I've been through. But maybe I'm not being fair about the

22

past, and I'm going at this whole thing with a chip on my shoulder . . . "

Andrea's voice trailed off and we allowed her some quiet moments to deal with the discomfort that had resulted from this unexpected glimpse of herself. Then we moved on to other things she should keep in mind as she began the program. Since it was obvious that Andrea had little patience for casual dating and was ready for a committed relationship, our screening of male clients for the same intentions would be very helpful to her. We reminded her, however, that the male's readiness for bonding usually needs a gentle approach, rather than a "ready or not" challenge. Everyone has a somewhat different definition of commitment these days, and to assume that any two people mean exactly the same thing by it is usually a mistake. For mature adults, the discussion of commitment can begin early in a relationship, but it should commence and continue as a search for a mutual focus. Both people must cultivate as much tenderness, patience, and empathy as possible for that search to develop into a practical and passionate agreement about the future.

In our face-to-face meeting with Andrea, we did our best to help her take on the responsibility for being fair and learning to judge in a balanced way the "pros and cons" of the men she would meet. After all, she would never meet Mr. Right if she remained obsessed on what was "wrong" with every candidate (or with men in general). We encouraged her to talk frankly with friends about how she appeared to people, hoping that trusted feedback would help her gain a more realistic view of herself over the long term. The cathartic glimpse of herself she had experienced in our office had been a start, but *she would need to do more to propel herself into the permanent attitude changes she needed in order to find a rewarding, permanent relationship.*

As Andrea's program progressed, we talked with her after each introduction, helping her reflect on her reactions and sort out what she did like about the men from what she didn't. As we expected, she was always better at criticism than positive appreciation, but over the next few months she did become noticeably more open, kind, and realistic, and a little less quick to judge. As she relaxed and learned more about herself and her real needs, Andrea's inner warmth, previously discernible only through the armor of her biting humor, gradually began to shine through on its own. As it did, Andrea developed a strong relationship with Matthew, another attorney and her fourth prospect in the program. The last we heard from them was a postcard from their home together in Boston, where Andrea found a new job and Matthew agreed to accompany her.

Will they stay together? Who knows? As with any relationship we have no way of predicting. But the Andrea who met Matthew has a far better chance at happiness than the Andrea who entered our office, who wasn't all there because she was so heavily defended.

*Again and again, we have to remind people that they must shed their suspicions and relinquish their fantasies if they hope to find a loving partner for life. You can't be settling a score or looking for heaven on earth. The starting point must be a willingness to take a serious look at **your** strengths and weaknesses, and to learn how others perceive **you**. The more you're willing to learn about yourself along* *the path of your search, the more rapidly will all the seeming obstacles fall away.*

STAYING OUT OF TROUBLE

Not long ago we overheard a conversation between two men in their early forties that seemed to sum up the way a lot of single people are feeling about the search for love these days. One man asked the other how work was going and the second man replied, "Just fine." Then the first man asked, "And how's your social life?"

The answer was a short, sharp laugh and a vigorous headshake. "Pretty awful. Between this AIDS thing and the way women feel about guys nowadays, well . . . Let's just say I'm not going out every night, okay?" The other man nodded and said, "Hey, I know what you mean." Grinning, his companion then replied, "Probably good for me, though. Keeps me out of trouble."

If you're a single person interested in finding a committed relationship and wondering where all the good men or women have gone, there's part of your answer: They're trying to stay out of trouble. Afraid of disease, wary of danger, and wearied by unfulfilling or disastrous relationship experiences, many fine people with a lot of love to give are psychologically barricading themselves from the attention of potential mates.

The paradox is that there have never been so many single people trying to meet each other. Of the 79 million adults that the U.S. Census Bureau identifies as widowed, divorced, or never married, it can be reasonably estimated that at least 30 million of them are searching seriously for a mate.* The evidence of their hunt is everywhere. The "personals" that used to appear only in weekly newspapers can now be found in daily papers and all kinds of professional and general-interest periodicals; electronic versions such as "telephone matching" are growing rapidly in popularity. Video-dating services, numbering in the thousands nationwide, have become a growth industry in recessionary times. The "lonely hearts club" of the past has become an instant-access electronic network, but no one has detected a boom in marriages or committed relationships as a result.

So it would seem that modern technology has made it easier than ever for people to get in touch with each other. We believe that the real problem is that people don't know how to touch, and really be touched, once they have met. The barricades of their fears, expectations, and fantasies are always getting in the way.

VOICES FROM THE SEARCH

Before surveying some of the most common obstacles, let's listen to how they are revealed in the voices of people who are actually out there looking for love. Later in this chapter, we'll look at some similar problematic attitudes we hear in the voices of our clients. The following personal ads were culled from just one West Coast singles newspaper, but they portray a wide range of the attitudes and desires of singles in the '90s. See if you can detect some of the ways in

---

*Some estimates of the "singles market" range as high as 66 million people. Our experience tells us that not all of the people who say they are looking for a mate are really serious about finding a committed relationship. We estimate that 90 percent of the women are, and 60 percent of the men.

which people may be blocking the very intimacy they desire.

WF, 28, looks like a model and looking for a prince of a guy who's ready to carry her away. Let's not get too serious . . .

BF, law student has one night a week to go out with a guy who can turn too little time into quality time . . .

WF, shapely, 35, looking for serious gentleman to share life with. Really tired of men who fear the "C" word . . .

Latin beauty, 27, to spice up your life. Help! I am tired of working and my parents want to know when I'm getting married . . .

WF, 40, in shape, wants a man who is ready to get down to the business of working our minds and bodies. I am successful in my business but I need more . . .

WM, beach bum, 35, I like the waves and the sun. I'm seeking a woman, curvy and has to look good in almost anything . . .

BM, attractive man ready for traditional relationship—no feminists, men haters, or rule breakers. It's my kingdom and I am the ruler . . .

WM, sports-minded blond looking for a woman who appreciates Monday night football, a cold beer, and hunting. Are you out there? . . .

WM, doctor with lots of interests wants a woman who

can appreciate the hard work it takes to practice medicine. Willing to give quality time to the woman who doesn't need a lot of reassurance . . .

WM, auto enthusiast, loves fast women who know how to spend money and make life exciting . . .

FAST WOMEN, FAST MEN TOO

What are the major barriers to intimacy that such voices are revealing? First, the very existence of personal ads is evidence of the **accelerated lifestyles** that influence us to rely on superficial information in meeting and getting to know people. Clients often present us with "laundry lists" of the characteristics they desire in a mate, assuming that we can quickly find a match that fits most of their immediate wants. Can't we just fix them up on the computer? Time is always short, it seems.

But the fact is that connection, romance, and commitment take lots of "quality" time. Finding a mate is not a matter of matching up want lists in the most efficient manner possible. It is instead an elaborate and unpredictable dance whose every step requires care, attention, and enthusiasm. The mating ritual was easier in earlier times, when the pace of life was slower and social communities were more closely knit than in our large urban centers. Our frequent **lifestyle transitions** and **cultural rootlessness** make it difficult to get to know people over a long period of time, and many of the social cues and clues that would be present in a closer community are eliminated in today's ever-changing, fast-paced urban environments.

Of course, our lifestyles are accelerated most often by **career demands**, which people increasingly experience as competing for the time and attention they would like to give to their search for intimate relationship. Typically, men in our culture have been most likely to put their careers ahead of love and family, but the increasing autonomy and equality of women have resulted in varying degrees of **role model confusion** affecting both genders. Men still aren't used to relating to women who are as successful as they are, or more so. As one anxious fellow put it recently, "If I make $30,000 and she makes $30,000, who's going to make the decisions in our relationship?" (Obviously it has not occurred to him that decision making can be a collaborative process!) On their side, women suffer anxiety that they must devote all their energy to keeping their hard-earned positions in the workplace, and that their very success may make them intimidating.

Entangled with this issue of changing roles at work are all the controversies of **sexual politics**, especially the question of what constitutes sexual harassment in the workplace. The anger and suspicions that surround such sensitive issues cannot help but spill over into social relations outside the office, influencing individuals of both genders to conclude that they might be safer keeping to themselves in a hermetic lifestyle.

LOOKING FOR MR. GOODLOOKS

One more social barrier that has to be mentioned is our **cultural focus on appearances**. Constantly bolstered by the entertainment media and advertising, the prejudice toward an ideally handsome or beautiful appearance makes it difficult for people to connect on the basis of their interior (and lasting) qualities. A prospective male client once offered to make our job a lot easier by sending us some photos clipped from *Playboy* to use as a guide in selecting his matches. John not only told him, "No thanks," but further suggested that he'd be wasting his time and money with us if he wasn't willing to consider a shift in his priorities.

It's our opinion that men or women who focus primarily on physical attributes simply don't understand their own nature and long-range needs very well. This superficial self-understanding will lead them to search only for attractive mates, without evaluating personality and character issues. That's a recipe for unhappy relationships, bad marriages, and bitter divorces.

We test for this tendency by asking clients to provide us with a list of the "top ten" attributes they would like a mate to have. If more than three of those attributes are physical, we have reason to suspect that the client presently has a low potential for bonding. It's not unusual to see men struggle to come up with nonphysical attributes that they desire. While we do give our clients general verbal information on the physical characteristics of match prospects, we do not provide photos of potential matches. We stress that people must get together on the basis of common interests, lifestyles, values, and goals, not mere physicality.

Julie once described a prospective match to a woman over the phone, who was delighted with everything she heard about the man until Julie mentioned that he had a moustache. "Oh no," the woman said. "No way. I hate men with moustaches. Let's go on to the next one."

"Wait a minute," Julie said. "I don't think you're

being very fair. Since everything else sounds good, don't you think you could put up with his moustache long enough to meet him and talk for a while?"

"But what if I like him, and he doesn't want to shave off his moustache?" the woman replied, sounding already indignant at the prospect. Julie had an answer at the ready: "Well, what if you fall in love and he decides to shave it off for you? Or what if you decide it's not really so important after all? Does a moustache matter so much that you'd turn away a good man because of it?"

Again and again, we find that men or women who have rigid or extreme requirements for physical appearance in a mate are really afraid of intimacy in one way or another, and are using appearance factors as a convenient barrier against finding the love they say they want. We're not psychologists, and we don't try to analyze what causes anyone to engage in such a self-defeating behavior. But we know from our practical experience that people can reorder their priorities and learn to look for what counts over the long term. Sometimes they merely need a reminder about what's really important. It's easy to lose your focus and common sense in the sensitive search for love.

THE INNER BARRIERS

The appearance issue demonstrates how the cultural barriers we've just looked at can be linked with internal, psychological factors. The inner barriers that people raise and then struggle against are as numerous and varied as the individuals themselves, but they can be typified in general terms. We'll be dealing with them at length throughout this book, but in shorthand form they can be summed up under five headings:

Inaccurate self-perceptions. This refers to people who have a very poor notion of how they appear to other people or of how they actually behave. "I'm forty-eight but everyone tells me I look thirty-five," or a similar boast, is something we hear often from middle-aged men. John calls that "malespeak" for "Give me a young bride!" Men may have indeed heard such compliments from their friends and relatives, who may be trying to make them feel more confident in their search for a relationship. But a more objective self-assessment is needed to help a man understand exactly how he appears to the women he meets.

Some people's inaccurate self-perceptions go in the opposite direction of vanity; they may believe they are too ugly or too uninteresting to attract anyone's attention. A significant portion of our work with people consists of helping them gain a realistic perception of themselves. A clearer self-image is reliably linked with a more realistic view of what is sought in a mate. We'll present some key approaches to the process of accurate self-perception in Chapter 3.

Self-sabotage. This applies to a multitude of negative ideas and behaviors, including excessive cynicism about oneself and others. Andrea's case history at the beginning of this chapter is a showcase of self-sabotaging beliefs. Whenever someone expresses a fixed, antagonistic belief about how "they" are—"men are animals" or "women are only interested in my money"—you can bet that the person is turning some aspect of their own self-doubt into a negative opinion about others. The net result is the prolongation of their own loneliness.

The more serious and subtle forms of self-sabotage may require professional counseling to detect, decode, and correct. But we find that most people can learn to understand how they're hurting their chances if we gently point out their self-sabotaging beliefs and question their usefulness. With careful reflection on their attitudes and relationship histories, most people can learn to shed these self-imposed hurdles and move on to a more open view of others. We push our clients to assume that the motives of the next potential mate are pure. His or her problems will show themselves soon enough; there's no need to assume problems that may not be there.

The pursuit of fantasies. Often we find that we're in the business of providing "constructive disillusionment," that is, helping people distinguish between their fantasy lovers and the real people available for relationship in the everyday world. There's nothing wrong with having a romantic fantasy in itself, especially as a form of playful inspiration. But when it's used seriously as an ideal measurement that no ordinary human being could possibly satisfy, the result will be failure, bitterness, and a growing sense of isolation.

The typical signs of destructive fantasizing are usually quite clear to us. A male is most likely to describe the perfect combination of a sex kitten and a perfect mom, all rolled up into a "total woman." A female will give one version or another of the "white knight" fantasy, the dream lover who will carry her off into a much better world than the one she experiences daily, assuaging all her insecurities and not incidentally improving her financial situation. As a rule, the qualities that people believe only a fantasy lover can provide are generally the qualities they need to develop within themselves. Men often need to learn to be more tender, communicative, and sensual; women often have work to do with the issues of power, independence, and self-assurance.

Most people are consciously aware that their fantasies are unattainable. Clients frequently tell us, "Of course, I don't expect to find anyone who's perfect." Then they will turn around and reject prospect after prospect on the basis of one or two less-than-ideal traits. That's why we often suggest that clients give the people they meet second and third chances, and look for a "positive balance" when assessing someone's good and bad points. We'll talk about this process in more detail in Chapter 6, which presents the Wingo 51-80 Principle.

Excessive self-protection. This is chiefly an issue for women these days, although some men have certainly developed self-defensive behaviors. When we check back with people after their first dates with prospective matches, we often hear from men that the women they met spent a long time with their arms crossed over their chests—figuratively, if not literally—while sporting poker faces. Women, of course, have developed these defenses for a lot of good reasons, but they are often not considering their net effect. Good and gentle men can easily be discouraged by a woman's distancing behavior, while males driven by a need to "conquer" or dominate may be the only ones who make the effort to break through.

Despite the plethora of self-help books telling women exactly what to do and what not to do in particular situations or with different "types" of men, we believe there's no simple answer or fail-safe strategy for women who must walk the line between reasonable self-protection and emotional accessibility. It's all a matter of having balanced instincts, and the best way to develop these instincts is through careful self-observation, reflection on your past experiences, and ongoing dedication to self-respect. Strategies are not the answer; self-reliance is.

Impatience. Here we are on the subject of time again. People have become so accustomed to quick fixes and faxes that they tend to expect instant answers to the very biggest questions of life, such as "Who will be my lifelong partner?" From the late '60s until the last few years, one of the major symptoms of impatience was the rapid onset of sexual relations in developing relationships, either for the purpose of instant physical gratification (most often a male motive) or as a means of cementing emotional bonds prematurely (the typical female motive).

The spreading fear of sexually transmitted diseases is changing this pattern, but we believe that fear is always the lesser part of discretion. It's better to let sexual intimacy develop slowly out of respect for the natural growth of mutual trust and comfort. The same goes for the issues of commitment and starting a family; regardless of one's age or biological clock, rushing into major decisions is a risky proposition. We must acknowledge that people evolve toward intimacy and commitment at different speeds. Patience allows people to adjust to each other's evolution with a minimum of friction.

TWENTY COMMON ATTITUDES:
ARE YOU GETTING IN YOUR OWN WAY?

The external and internal obstacles we've reviewed show up in our clients in the guise of many different attitudes, prejudices, and suspicions. Whether they sound petty or profound to us, we know that people have come to these conclusions about people and relationships because of their personal experience. It's difficult to convince people that their convictions are possibly unjustified.

Instead, we try to help clients reflect on whether these attitudes are useful or harmful to them in their search for a mate. We often say something like, "You may want to reevaluate this idea you have that men (or women) are always (this or that). It might be getting in the way of meeting someone who's right for you." Then we wait and see whether the client takes the time to reflect on his or her assumptions. People who have decided to pay for advice and professional assistance are usually ready to consider a new way of looking at things, even if we have to confront them with an unpleasant realization or two.

Following is a list of twenty common attitudes (ten usually held by women, ten by men) that we've heard frequently in our client sessions. Some take the form of suspicions, others are non-negotiable demands. If any of these match your attitudes, pay special attention to our brief comentary following each point. Remember that the issue is not whether these attitudes are true or justifiable in your experience, but whether they actually serve you in your search for a mate. The attitudes marked with an asterisk (*) may be common to both genders.

Common Attitudes of Women

1. **"Most men are afraid of monogamy and commitment."**

Most? Who knows? The point is that many men *are* ready to commit. Our impression is that the men who are most aggressive in the singles arena are the same ones most likely to be "serial daters," looking to feed a need for attention or to add notches to their record of conquests. If women can learn to see through the games of the charmers and give the more reticent, lower-profile fellows a chance, they'll discover plenty of men who have a future in them.

2. **"Men will say or do anything for sex—basically they can't be trusted."**

True, men will generally place sex higher on their list of "immediate needs" than women will, but that does not always translate to "they can't be trusted." In recent years, this aspect of *vive la différence* has too often become a weapon in the battle of the sexes. We think that women can find ways to simultaneously appreciate and exert some control over the male species' ready interest in sexual activity. The first step is always to be open and direct, calling men on any unpleasant behavior right on the spot and politely suggesting more respectful ways to express and share sexual interest. Read Chapter 6, "From Dating to Relating," for tips on old-fashioned flirting, developing sexual discretion, and exercising good sexual etiquette. (And remember: Not all men are beasts!)

3. **"I can't show any tenderness or vulnerability because a man will take advantage of me. I need to look uninterested and not too available."**

Think again if you want to make a solid connection with a smart, sensitive guy. We believe that men instinctively seek a woman's natural femininity, softness, and vulnerability (not to be confused with weakness!). Constructing a chinkless defense is a good way to guarantee that no man will ever want to get close to you. He must feel that you don't have everything you need in life already; he needs to sense that his presence in a relationship will make a difference. You must feel your way toward a balance of strength and accessibility, reservation and openness.

4. **"Men will be threatened by my professional success."**

Some will—the same men who will be threatened by your candor, your intelligence, your common sense, your grace under pressure. Do you really want to worry about attracting these men anyway? There are two ways to answer this concern: Look for men at your "success level" or above, or look for men with a self-confident "I'm okay" stance no matter what they've achieved. Men who fit the latter description may be rarer, but they are the best bets for long-term bonding.

5. **"I need a successful, wealthy man. He must make at least $$$ a year."**

The numbers game is always a recipe for disaster. You're better off looking for qualifiers like self-respect, dedication to growth and self-improvement, and a healthy lifestyle. Wealth is neither good nor evil in itself; it's a person's attitude toward it that counts. And when defining success, remember the factors of health, happiness, and fulfillment that really round it out. If you think all this is poppycock because you've already given up on love and mutual respect, and are willing to settle for a sugar daddy—well, we can't help you. You're on your own in a more tragic way than you probably know.

6. **"Men really don't want an equal, 50/50 relationship; they prefer to dominate."**

You're hanging out with the wrong generation. We think men have grown tremendously in the last twenty years, at least the well-educated and most perceptive ones. Look for the guys who don't flinch or foam at the mouth when they hear feminist sentiments. That doesn't mean they all have to be like Alan Alda, just that they've given women's concerns over the last twenty years a serious hearing. Maybe you should abandon the local bar and try a coffee shop at the nearest university campus.

7. **"I have to look great because men don't pay attention to anything but a woman's looks."**

Sure, it's important to look your best because first impressions do count for something. But what's most important to a man who will care about you is simply the evidence that *you know how to take care of yourself*. So don't overdo the wardrobe or makeup. It's so much better simply to be clean, appropriately dressed, and at peace with yourself than to be tottering in high heels, masked by rouge and mascara, and constantly pulling down a too-short skirt. Excessive and overt attention to your looks or apparel can be a red flag that signals poor self-esteem and a low potential for long-term bonding. If you want to meet superficial men, however, that's the way to do it.

8. **"I'm not going to waste time talking to a man who doesn't want children."**

If you want kids and a prospective fellow makes it clear on the first or second date that he absolutely does not, then you'll probably want to shake hands and move on. But don't be too quick to judge someone who merely expresses doubt or reluctance about children. Most men will probably consider having children with the right mate, if all the factors of a loving relationship are in place. Just make sure you're not exerting excessive pressure because of your own urges or biological clock. No man likes to feel that he's just a sperm bank.

*9. **"He has to be 'into' skiing/ballet/the arts/working out."**

Replace "into" with "open to" and you'll greatly improve your chances for finding a playful and flexible partner. Someone who happens to mirror your interests may not actually be as interesting in the long run as someone from a completely different world who demonstrates the capacity to try out new ideas and adventures. He could have something fun and challenging for you to try as well.

*10. **"He has to be Jewish/Catholic/born again/a believer in crystals."**

Again, a good mate primarily needs to be open and tolerant of a wide variety of ideas and influences, be they religious, political, or cultural. If you're going to limit your search to followers of a particular religious belief or sect, then don't be resentful if you encounter slim pickings. We think it's much wiser to look for the *innate spiritual qualities* that transcend religious beliefs, such as humility, compassion, and wonder. Respect for all the differences that may be present in a partnership is absolutely required. If you cherish the potential you have for teaching and learning from each other, your differences will be a source of mutual stimulation rather than conflict. If it's your family or friends who are pressuring you to find a mate of a particular religious or political persuasion, it may be necessary for you to pose the question, "Whose life (and love) are we talking about, anyway?"

Common Attitudes of Men

1. **"Women don't trust men's goals going into a relationship."**

This has some basis in fact because so many men look for sexual relations too early in a relationship. But the answer to this is not to assume that a woman doesn't trust you right off the bat; the answer is to be trustworthy and patient. Be a good guy and show your enthusiasm for her without being pushy or defensive. Women cherish the gentleness in a strong man who can wait and respect a woman's need to approach intimacy only after trust is realized.

2. **"Women like taller men."**

Some do, some don't; most don't care as long as more important qualities are apparent, like honesty, reliability, and self-confidence, both physical and emotional. Like all the obsessions about physicality (breast size, penis length, and so on), this one is exaggerated. Make sure you're getting your information about what women like directly from the kind of women you respect—not just from other guys, advertising, or stand-up comics.

3. "Women like macho, demonstrably 'strong' men."

Or so macho men would like to believe. In fact, women value a man's strength most when it is not necessary for him to show it. A woman wants to feel that a man has the capacity to take care of her (and their children), but she is likely to be repulsed by a man with a constant need to show off and prove himself. If she is attracted to macho displays, it's probably because she doesn't trust her own strength as a woman. If you really want a lifelong partner who's weak and overly dependent, go ahead and strut your stuff.

4. "Women don't really like sex."

We try to break the news gently to any man who reveals this attitude, but it's just plain wrong. Women have always liked good, *sensitive* sex. It wasn't always socially acceptable to admit it until the advent of feminism, but men can be thankful that women are now much more explicit about what excites and satisfies them. What women don't like is fast, insensitive "me first" sex. When men have consistently unpleasant sexual experiences because they're not paying enough attention to their intimate partners, they often develop this cop-out in order to excuse their own behavior.

5. "I need to impress her with my success/income/ physicality/social skills."

The problematic word here is "impress." Parading your strong points too early in a social encounter will often accomplish exactly the opposite of what you intend. An intelligent woman may be alerted to your sense of inadequacy or lack of integrity. The temptation to self-advertise is one reason we recommend "side-by-side" rather than "face-to-face" activities for first and second dates—seeing a movie or play, joining in group recreation, or people watching in a public place. It's helpful to have something else going on in your environment that you can focus on during a first date, to take the pressure off the tendency to "grill" each other or rush an intimacy you don't naturally feel yet. Don't push too hard for the face-to-face, heart-to-heart talks; they will come soon enough. More on this in Chapter 5, "Across a Crowded Room."

6. **"Women are only looking for men with money."**
Some are, but they're pretty easy to spot. Listen for excessive flattery, lots of indirect questions about your income, and overt manipulation. Then stop watching the prime-time soap operas and meet the women in the real world. Most women want a man who has enough on the ball to be fiscally responsible and on his way to making something of himself, not necessarily making a fortune. If a woman wants to have a family and intends not to work or to stop her career to do so, she will naturally be looking for a man with a solid financial profile. But any woman presenting non-negotiable financial demands is not interested in a real relationship anyway. If you seem to be meeting a lot of gold diggers, take a look in the mirror and check out how you're presenting yourself. If you're showing off your wealth, what kind of attention did you expect to attract?

7. **"Single women over thirty-five are hard and embittered."**
Many women over thirty-five do give this impression. They've come to this state for some good reasons: They've been jilted, lied to, and used. The fact is that men nowa-

days do have to make up for the sins of their brothers, but that doesn't mean you have to feel guilty for something you didn't do. All you need to do is be understanding, patient, and empathetic.

An equation to keep in mind with highly defended women (or anyone else who's been emotionally wounded, for that matter) is that "Patience = Respect." We know from working with defensive women that there is almost always a warm, caring, and sensitive person under the surface armor. Show her the respect she's seen too little of in the last ten years, and she'll come out for you. If she doesn't show signs of relaxing after a reasonable length of time, there may be something going on that you don't want to get involved in.

*8. "Anyone over forty who hasn't been married is a terrible risk. Something must be wrong with them."

Or perhaps they've been away on a long archaeological expedition, wrapped up in writing the Great American Novel, or discovering the cure for cancer. More likely, the never-married, forty-plus person has been through one or two long-term, monogamous relationships that were equivalent to a marriage. The point is that you don't know why someone hasn't been married until you ask. As with so many of the assumptions and stereotypes that people bring into our office, this one only serves the purpose of narrowing a person's field of possibilities. If someone can eventually narrow down their possibilities to none at all, then they can excuse themselves from the scary search for love and commitment entirely! We see this kind of maneuvering all the time.

*9. "Women prefer outgoing, gregarious men. They don't like shy, introverted guys like me."

Another generalization often used to excuse oneself from the hunt. Men sometimes come up with this idea because they've been looking in the wrong places for a woman who would appreciate their quiet nature. Or they're drawn to outgoing women because they wish they were more social themselves.

We have always felt that extreme opposites attract divorce; rarely will deeply introverted and wildly sociable types maintain a healthy, long-term relationship. What the introvert first finds exciting in the extrovert soon becomes frenetic and irritating; on the other side, the serenity that the quiet one provides for the party person eventually becomes a crushing boredom. The key is to look for someone who can balance your social style but is not at the far opposite end of the spectrum. If someone is *too* fascinating in this regard, watch out—fascination wears off.

*10. "I have to affect a certain style during my first few dates to get a woman's attention. I won't get anywhere just being me."

It's hard for the insecure to believe, but "be yourself" always works best—especially these days, when people in the dating arena are becoming more and more suspicious of strangers and their motives. To be less than honest or straightforward is to be a stranger *to yourself.* Intelligent people will pick up on the subtle signals of deception even if they don't know exactly what's going on. The result is always rejection. Better to stumble into a first date and make a complete fool of yourself than to affect a style that sets off alarms in the other person's head. Who knows—it may be precisely your willingness to reveal your imperfections that helps you make a solid, heartfelt connection.

OUR SECRET

If you've consulted other matchmaking books before this one, you know that there are many different approaches to the kind of work we do. One recent book claims that the most important factor in seeking a mate is making sure that your "birth order" (whether you were born first, last, or in the middle of your siblings) is compatible with that of a potential mate. Another offers the principles of cognitive therapy in order to help readers become psychologically prepared for a committed relationship. Yet another, written by one of our matchmaking colleagues, provides women with a detailed strategic approach that suggests, among many other things, "Don't *play* hard to get, *be* hard to get," and "Be love stingy."

Our basic approach does not depend on deep psychologizing or lengthy strategizing. In fact, we have only one matchmaking "strategy" that might be called the secret of our success. We don't mind giving it away right here in the second chapter of this book, because we think it's a philosophy that needs to be more widely heard and applied. We'll restate it in many different ways throughout the course of this book, but it can be summed up this way:

> Getting to know and trust yourself is the foundation for finding a lifetime mate. Be prepared to work hard on communication and openness. Think deeply and speak openly about what commitment means to you.

That's it. This advice may sound simple, but it's demanding to put into practice and follow consistently. We think it's easier to keep in mind than a hundred piecemeal strategies or a complex psychological theory, and so it's likely to stay with you longer.

If we've done our job right, this philosophy will have become a part of you by book's end. We've tried to present our perspective in an entertaining and optimistic way, and we've included our personal history as a committed, imperfect, and still-learning couple whenever we think it might be useful. Should you actually find this book inspiring, then our fondest hopes will be realized.

And if you have turned to us for advice because the search for love has gotten you frazzled, fearful, and frustrated, let us say this: Calm down! It's not so bad out there, and our bet is that you're a more appealing person with more to offer than you think. You don't need to come up with a foolproof strategy or plug into the largest possible data base in order to find your mate for life. You do need to give yourself permission to let your authentic, vulnerable, giving, and irreplaceable self out into the world. This way, you'll find a lasting love a lot sooner than you may currently think possible.

3

Who Are You?
What Do You Want?
And What Do You Really Need?

Love is, above all, the gift of oneself.
—Jean Anouilh

From the moment that Louise shook hands with us, it was easy to see that she was a kind and cheerful woman. Her warm brown eyes peeked out from underneath a broad-brimmed, floral sun hat that was just eccentric enough to get one's attention, and her smile was bright and sweet. Compared to the majority of people who come into our office with noticeable anxiety, Louise seemed to bring along her own atmosphere of optimism and goodwill. In terms of friendliness and approachability, she would obviously have a head start on most single women in her age bracket of the mid-fifties.

What we also noticed immediately about Louise was that she didn't quite fit her description of herself. Over the phone, she'd told us that she was 5'4", weighed 140 pounds, and thus might be seen as "a little overweight. But I work out regularly and I'm really just solidly built," she had as-

serted. In fact, she looked at least twenty pounds heavier than she reported, and the weight was obviously not due to over-training. To our experienced matchmaking eyes, this obvious discrepancy was problematic. Whenever someone's self-description is noticeably skewed from observable reality, we know that our job is going to be more difficult.

But Louise gave us little time to worry about that. In an ebullient, take-charge tone of voice, she was soon rattling off her list of expectations for a prospective husband—who would be her third, after two divorces. "Now that the kids are completely on their own," she said, "my needs have changed and I want to find a mature, responsible man who respects that. There's lots of things I want to do before I get too old, so I don't want some old fuddy-duddy who doesn't want to have any fun. I know that most men my age will have some kids, which I don't mind as long as they're grown." Louise chuckled and said, "My career as a mom is definitely over."

We smiled and nodded. Julie asked, "Would you like to have another kind of career now? What are some of those things you'd like to do with a new man in your life?"

Louise shrugged matter-of-factly and said, "Well, I'd like to travel, of course. I'd like to spend about a year in Europe, and I've always wanted to go to Australia." Her eyes danced with anticipation, and it occurred to John that Louise's implicit message to a prospective marriage partner probably went something like "Love me, love my itinerary." Silently scanning a row of male candidates in his mind's eye, John was already dismissing a few who would be unlikely to respond positively to such an upfront demand. Truth to tell, most of the men in the Wingo files would opt out of meeting Louise once they heard about her Rubenesque-plus figure.

Julie's attention was caught by something else. "If you don't mind my asking, Louise, what's your income from your real estate job? Is that a full-time thing?"

For the first time Louise reacted a little nervously, as if there was something she wanted to hide. "Oh no," she replied hurriedly. "I don't like traipsing all over the place enough to do real estate full time. I work a couple days a week and I do all right. With the money I get from Frank and Jeremy, I'm comfortable. I'm not saying things couldn't be better, of course. I don't particularly like living in an apartment, even though mine is spacious. I'd like to have a nice house to decorate, and a big sunny studio for my painting."

Still distracted by his mental review of steadily vanishing candidates, John didn't catch all of Louise's response to Julie. But the end of her wish list got his attention. He sensed there was something else this lady wasn't being perfectly candid about. He locked eyes with her and asked directly, "Louise, do you have any feelings about what kind of money you'd want your next husband to be making? Do you have any expectations in that area?"

Louise's perpetual smile faded and she started to fuss with the strap on her oversized pocketbook. "Well, not really," she said distractedly, looking away from John's gaze. "I mean, of course he should be a man of some accomplishment."

Uh-oh. Now the cat was out of the bag: Louise was really looking for a gentleman with pretty big bucks, someone whose largesse would allow her to quit work and spend her time pursuing more aesthetic tasks at home—whenever she wasn't globe-trotting with her new, well-heeled beau. While we're not in the business of passing moral judgment on our clients' desires, we do know how important it is that people are honest with themselves, and us, about their priorities. They must also face the facts about the kind of priorities that foster love and commitment, and the kind that result in disappointment, disharmony, and divorce.

Now Louise had three apparent strikes against her in matchmaking terms: overweight, an indirectness that sometimes lapsed into outright dishonesty, and simple greed. John was watching the cast of male candidates in his head dwindle down to zero, wondering if it was time for J. Wingo International to bow out politely from a probably impossible mission. But Julie, usually the more sanguine of the two of us, proceeded with the interview by asking Louise to describe her two previous marriages.

Frank was the man Louise had met in college, married, and raised their son and daughter with. She had fond memories of their romance and first few years together, when she had supported Frank through law school. "Frank was a great organizer," Louise recalled in an admiring tone. "He planned exactly when we should start having children, where we could afford to live until his career got off the ground, and a lot of other decisions that always seemed to have perfect timing. I quit working at the bank when Joshua was born, and we moved into the big house when Laurel came along. I guess we were the standard American family," Louise said with a warm smile. "But I was a good mother. You can just ask my kids."

"You don't have to convince me," Julie replied. "I can

hear it in your voice. You told me over the phone that your family is still close, and you feel like Frank is a good friend now. Still, though, you two got divorced. Can you tell us what happened to bring on the breakup?"

Louise's face darkened. "Well, things just seemed to change when Laurel was in her last year of high school. Josh was already off to college. Frank had been a full partner at his firm for five or six years, and I thought we were on top of the world, I really did. I was looking forward to the two of us traveling when both kids were out of the house and Frank could slow down his schedule a little bit."

At this point Louise's words slowed dramatically and her voice became quieter. She was obviously treading on a territory of pain. "But Frank got . . . I don't know, dissatisfied with me. He said I was letting myself go. I mean, I had gained a little weight since college, like most people! But it seemed like he didn't want to be around me if he didn't have to be. I figured it was some kind of mid-life crisis. I braced myself for him having an affair."

"Did you get any counseling together?" Julie asked.

"Oh, no," Louise said with a tight smile. "I mean, I talked a lot to an old friend of mine, and she was really helpful. But Frank didn't believe in therapy back then. His attitude was that you are who you are, and you just have to live with it." She paused and smiled ruefully. "Strangely enough, Frank did go into counseling just recently, and he says a whole new world is opening up for him. I'm glad about that. I just wish it had happened a little earlier."

Julie nodded and asked very quietly, "Did Frank ever have an affair?"

53

Oddly, Louise brightened and returned to her normal, cheery tone. "Oh, a bunch—if you can even call them affairs. I don't know how long he had already been going out with different young secretaries before we split, but nothing ever lasted longer than a few dates. Frank has, well, some sexual problems. Poor baby, he's still bouncing around from relationship to relationship with all these younger women, almost ten years after our divorce. Now he comes over to talk about his problems—can you imagine? My God, I feel like his mother now!"

We both watched with fascination as Louise's expressions flickered back and forth between genuine sympathy and a perverse satisfaction about Frank's problems. But we knew she had been through a second, brief marriage that she didn't seem interested in talking about. John took the initiative: "What's the story on your second marriage, Louise? What was your relationship with Jeremy like?"

Louise stiffened a little; John always seemed to be asking the hard questions. "Jeremy was an acquaintance of Frank's, to tell the truth. Really more of an opponent; they faced off in court a lot. Anyway, I met Jeremy at a cocktail party about a year after the divorce. I'd gone with some girlfriends of mine to this party that I knew Frank would be invited to also, but I didn't want to play a game of avoiding him. As it turned out, he got wind I was coming and was too embarrassed to show up with his little girlfriend at the time." Louise grinned broadly. We could see that she would drift back to the subject of Frank at every opportunity.

"What did you first like about Jeremy?" Julie persisted.

"Well, he was very successful!" Louise exclaimed, and

*upon catching John's eye added, "and so charming. He's Eng-
lish, you know, very classy in an old-world kind of way. We
did a lot of fun things together at first, including the trip to
England just before we were married. He promised we would
do a lot of traveling like that, but . . . " Louise looked long-
ingly out the window for a second before resuming her train of
thought. "Well, it just didn't work out that way."*

*"Do you mean that things changed after you were mar-
ried?" Julie asked.*

*"They certainly did!" Louise snapped. "It was a full
year before we went away again—down to Rio—and then
we had to leave after just a few days because he had an emer-
gency at work. I did have fun for a while fixing up his house.
It was really stunning, and he'd only had a housekeeper there
since his wife died and his son moved to England. He had to
entertain a lot, and he did give me a lot of appreciation for
all the dinner parties I put together. But after a couple years,
it got old."*

*"It sounds like he expected you to keep that up indefi-
nitely," Julie sympathized.*

*"Yes, I'm afraid so. Besides the parties, he was home less
and less as time went on. I guess he was more successful than
Frank because he worked even more. And he was so cut-and-
dried, it gave me the shivers sometimes. When I finally complained that I felt more like a social director on his payroll
than a wife, his reaction was to draw up the divorce papers!"
Louise's indignant expression faded to a thin smile as she
added, "Of course, he was very generous with the settlement."*

*By now, it was becoming clear that Louise had come to
us looking for professional assistance in committing the same*

kind of error she'd made in her second marriage. Never having experienced a truly close, supportive relationship with Frank, she had simply opted for a bigger wallet when she remarried. She mistook Jeremy's style and success for qualities that would guarantee a stable, secure relationship, and was disillusioned to realize that he had indeed "hired" her to fulfill a secondary role in his status-oriented life.

Paradoxically, Louise and Frank were now becoming the kind of friends they had never been in marriage. But there was no longer enough attraction and too much old hurt between them to enable a reunion as intimate partners. If we were going to take Louise into the program, we would have to counter her tendency to look for financiers of the lifestyle she would like to become accustomed to. We'd also have to try nudging her toward a recognition of the nonmaterial qualities of friendship and mutual respect that give any relationship a lasting foundation.

Also, Louise needed to learn how to better gauge the compatibility of goals between her and a prospective mate, a factor that's particularly important for relationships forming in the second half of life. A man Louise could have fun with would probably have to be a man obsessed neither by money nor career, which means he probably wouldn't be rich.

John thought Louise's chances in the program were slight, partly because he's pessimistic about most men's capacity to deemphasize physical factors in their prospective partners. But Julie was impressed by Louise's sunny nature, open-minded curiosity, and general optimism—all strong positive qualities that are often missing in divorced women of Louise's age. Julie prevailed.

After unsuccessful dates with her first few prospects—whom she disdained partly because they were not wealthy men, a deliberate choice on our part—Louise connected with Hank, a sixty-year-old university professor. Hank's respectable salary barely topped Louise's income from her various sources. But he had a wide-ranging curiosity to match hers, and Louise reported back to us that she had never met a man who seemed so interested in her as a person. Hank wanted to travel, too, it turned out. He just wanted to do it in a little more challenging style than Louise was accustomed to. The last time we heard from Louise, she was going with Hank to buy her first hiking boots. It sounded like she was finally going to start getting the "regular workout" she had claimed in her first phone call.

FACING THE FACTS

Louise's story illustrates one of the fundamental problems that drives up the divorce rate and keeps many singles shuttling in and out of brief, unsatisfying relationships: *What people think they want in a mate is often not what they really need.* Louise thought she wanted another wealthy man to set her up in a privileged lifestyle, but in fact she'd already been married twice to men who had plenty of money, with unsatisfying results.

Although her first marriage was certainly not a total loss, there was a tragic element to it: Frank and Louise had raised a family without ever becoming intimate, supportive friends. Like many men in our culture, Frank focused so much attention on his career that he delayed crucial parts of his growing up until an inevitable mid-life crisis, during which he finally began to show more of his emotional vulnerability to Louise. By that time, however, they were divorced, and Louise had to settle for being a maternal chum to her ex-husband. Having married Jeremy partly out of revenge, she had discovered that his superior wealth, status, and sophistication translated into even less intimacy than she had known with Frank.

What was hard for Louise to recognize was that continuing to look mostly for money in a potential mate would exacerbate her problems, rather than buy her the lifestyle she imagined would be heaven on earth. Globe-trotting, an unlimited budget for interior decorating, and a sunny painting studio were not her deepest needs. Mutual respect, a shared sense of enjoying life, and fair, intimate communication with a mate were more on target. We could help Louise partly by steering her toward interesting men who didn't devote their lives to money, but ultimately she was the one who had to change her priorities. On this and other levels, Louise had to start facing the facts about who she really was.

At the end of the last chapter, we said that our secret has a lot to do with urging people to get to know and trust themselves. If that was a simple matter, this book would already be over. But the subject gets more complicated when you recognize that we all have a tendency to deceive ourselves about our most obvious flaws and problems.

Louise, for instance, liked to believe she weighed 140 pounds when it would be apparent to anyone that she probably topped 160. While being overweight definitely reduces one's chances for finding a mate in our culture—especially and unfairly for women, it must be said—a more serious obstacle is not being able to talk about it straightforwardly. We think the recent anti-diet backlash is a healthy movement in this regard, in that it's encouraging anyone with a weight problem to acknowledge their condition openly. Then one can accept it as a permanent feature and deal with the consequences, or commit to the long-term lifestyle changes that really make a difference in weight control. We'll have more to say about this very sensitive subject shortly.

HOW MUCH SELF-KNOWLEDGE DO YOU NEED?

When it comes to facing the facts about oneself for the purpose of finding a committed relationship, the question above is crucial. In psychological or spiritual terms, there's no end to self-knowledge, but that's not what we're here to talk about. We're neither therapists nor gurus. We *are* experienced specialists in the unpredictable business of arranging contacts for the purpose of long-term, committed partnerships. From observing hundreds of people going through the emotionally challenging search for relationship, we've learned what we think constitutes *practical self-knowledge* on certain key factors of our common human experience.

In this chapter, we'll look at those factors from two perspectives:

1. How realistic are you about yourself?
   and
2. What do you really need in a mate?

Notice that these are both *self-assessment perspectives*; the difference is that the first "looks within" and the second "looks out from within." It's important to understand that our list of factors for both kinds of self-assessment stops at an arbitrary cut-off point. We could have gone on forever in increasing detail about more and more factors of self-knowledge, but we wanted to give you just enough to think about without encouraging self-obsession or navel gazing. If you reflect carefully on what we have to say and try on the questions we bring up, we think you'll have a pretty good handle on how much self-knowledge you need to smooth the search ahead of you. An excellent way to sharpen your discrimination and alertness on that search is to question things you're told that don't seem to ring true— so don't take what we say as matchmaking gospel. Just try it on for size.

HOW REALISTIC ARE YOU ABOUT YOURSELF?

In our interviews with clients, we often use our eyes, ears, and experience to help "re-set" people's view of themselves to a more realistic self-perception. We can generally predict which aspects of a person will prove favorable or problematic to another in a first-date setting. Most people cannot recognize the same aspects in themselves. In this section, we want to give you some questions, challenges, and provocative ideas that may help you do some re-setting of your self-perception on your own. If this process is sometimes disconcerting, remember that the goal is to build your honesty, confidence, and appeal *based on who you really are,* not on pretenses. No matter how romantic or intriguing they may seem in the short term, relationships between pretenders don't last very long, and generally end in deception, fraud, and pain.

The five major factors for self-assessment are:

Physical attractiveness
Openness and approachability
Intelligence and education
Sense of humor
Communication skills

Before we get into them, let's look at some of the tools you might use to re-set your view of yourself in regard to these factors.

Tools for Self-Assessment

Besides thoughtful reflection, there are several ways you can learn to view yourself more realistically. They can all be used for most of the factors that will follow. One is to discuss the questions we'll be bringing up with a trusted friend or two, giving them carte blanche to be perfectly honest with you about their opinions: "Feel free to tell me what you really see in me, and don't worry about my feelings at the moment. I'm begging you to be truthful." Even with such permission, you should be aware that the closest of friends may tend to flatter or encourage you at times when a little confrontation might actually be more helpful. Relatives near your age may be a little more objective, as long as your relationship to them is not tinged with family tensions that might result in unfair prejudices.

The ideal peer consultant would be an acquaintance of the opposite sex, perhaps someone you know from work, whose opinion, maturity, and social skills you respect but who is not attractive to you as a prospect for intimate partnership. You might invite him or her out to dinner, or exchange some other favor in return for a few hours of honest opinions and advice about yourself. Try to be as serious and organized about this as possible. Come with your questions prepared in advance. Otherwise, you may lapse into a conversation that's interesting in its own right, but not very helpful to you in your search for a mate. (Unless, of course, you find that your peer consultant is attractive to you after all!)

Another method for self-assessment is to make your own matchmaking video—but keep it to yourself. Tape yourself talking about what's important to you in the search for relationship, perhaps answering some of the questions we raise, and then watch yourself with a caring and serious attitude. How do you appear physically? Are you sincere? Warm? Natural? If you're not comfortable speaking in front of a camera alone, tape a conversation between yourself and a friend or peer consultant.

It may take a few tries before you're comfortable enough to appear relaxed on camera, but what you learn from watching yourself may be well worth the effort. Just as it can be a shock the first time we hear our voice as others do on a tape recording, it can be very surprising to see how differently we look, speak, and behave before the objective eye of the camera, compared to how we *think* we appear. This may be the closest you can get to seeing yourself as others will see you, and can be particularly helpful for the physical and social aspects of self-assessment.

For the inner, more psychological aspects, you may find it helpful to start a personal journal if you don't already keep one. Writing an autobiography with the goal of an intimate relationship in mind may help you sort out some of the past problems and prejudices that may cloud your view of self and others in the present. You can also keep a thoughtful record of your experiences in meeting people, taking care to go deeper than "just the facts" or first impressions. As we noted in Chapter 2, our accelerated lifestyles tend to encourage superficial ideas about who we are, and shallow perceptions of what other people are really like. Slowing yourself down enough to write and reflect on your feelings, desires, and experiences might improve your inner *and* outer vision just enough to prevent you from overlooking a worthy mate.

Self-Assessment Factors:
Physical Attractiveness

Women's looks get so much attention in our culture that we're going to turn the tables and pose a question about physical attractiveness first to men:

Do you know the single most important factor about your looks in the eyes of most women?

The answer may surprise you. In our experience, it's not just a hard or soft body, facial or head hair, expensive clothing, or, contrary to popular mythology, a bulge in your pants. In fact, most of the women we've met are sensitive to a man's personal *grooming* more than anything else. It's no secret that men can seem to get away with more sloppiness in public than women can (or care to). But men who are not paying a reasonable amount of attention to cleanliness and neatness are often turning off more women than they are aware of. As Julie says, "A woman can always dress a man

63

more attractively. But she seldom has a desire to clean him up." So if you're a man who thinks your ripped, dirty jeans are showing off your muscles to great advantage, you may want to think again.

For both men and women, grooming is a reflection of one's care for oneself. Too little grooming signals a kind of self-forgetting, or even dislike for oneself, on the inside. It may also mean that someone doesn't value a potential mate enough to present oneself in a pleasing way. Too much grooming—in the sense of trendy, expensive clothing, attention-grabbing hairdos, or heavy makeup—can signal self-obsession and a lack of available attention for other people. Women are sometimes driven to the use of excessive makeup and sexually provocative attire by an insecurity about their looks, an insecurity fed by advertising and other cultural expectations. Men are sometimes driven to purchase unnecessarily expensive clothing by putting more faith in a designer label than they have in themselves.

Whether you're male or female, the questions you need to ask yourself about grooming and dress are simple:

Is your appearance clean and neat?

Is your style of dress reasonably current and appropriate to the situation, whether it's work or play?

Do your friends or co-workers ever compliment your appearance? Do you have a good idea of what looks flattering on you?

How much time and money do you spend on your looks, excluding exercise? (If you spend more than a fourth of your budget or your free time on clothes and makeup—and you're not in the fashion industry—you're probably overgroomed!)

Apart from your genetic inheritance, are you comfortable with the way you look in public? Once you're dressed for an

evening out, are you able to forget about your appearance and con-
centrate on having a good time?

Finally, let's get back to the weight factor in physical attractiveness. As Julie says defiantly, "Women don't want to hear *one more word* about their weight!" Unfortunately, it's one of the first things men notice in assessing women they meet, and the greatest single factor by which most men (though certainly not all) exclude mating prospects from their view. We are often in the unpleasant position of telling women who are in the upper reaches of their medically approved weight range that they're probably a little too heavy to be attractive to most men. To catch a man's eye in our culture, women need to be on the thin side.

Though women are gradually becoming more sensitive to men's fitness and appearance, they are generally more accepting of a little paunch on a man if they like him on most other accounts. It would be healthier for men if their general attitude was similar, but that's not the case at the present time. We have to take the heat sometimes for reminding women of this double standard, but we have to be honest about how things are, not how they should be.

That's a good rule to follow for the overweight woman, too. Be honest about your weight and appearance when meeting men. If you like the way you are and don't want to change, say so. But be willing to accept that you may be decreasing your chances of finding a match. If you're unhappy with your shape and would like to lose weight, admit it and do something about it. It's our experience that the overweight women who are most excluded from the dating and mating arena are those who, like Louise, deny the obvious and try to make excuses for themselves. That raises the kinds of suspicions and uncertainty that John felt while talking to Louise. In such a case, men may say it's the weight that bugs them because it's plainer to see than the dishonesty and self-deception that's going on.

If it were possible to set an optimum standard of appearance for all men and women looking for mates, we would call it an honest, "low-key" beauty or handsomeness. Being too attractive to a large number of people can get you a lot of attention but very little in the way of a sustainable relationship, as you may tend to become a fantasy object for others. Or you may find it easy to bail out of relationships early when you know that there is always someone out there interested in you, if only superficially.

On the other hand, few people are born so absolutely unattractive that a healthy degree of self-acceptance shining through from inside fails to compensate for whatever God didn't give them. All in all, the single most important question you can ask yourself about your physical appearance is: *Are you taking care of yourself?* If not, how can you expect someone else to think you're worth caring about?

Self-Assessment Factors: Openness and Approachability

Are you a person toward whom others gravitate in a social event? Is there something in your smile, posture, or eyes that makes people feel free to come up and say, "Hi, how are you?" Are you comfortable with lightly touching your peers at work, or even strangers at a party, and being touched in a friendly, nonsexual way? Can you smile at yourself in a mirror and feel approval of what you see?

If you can answer these questions affirmatively, you

can assess yourself as an open and approachable person from the matchmaking perspective. One of the curious things we've observed about human nature is that most people don't have a good idea of how approachable they are, and are even surprised to be asked about it. People who are closed-off, cold, or distant from others are often mystified about why they don't meet anyone interesting in their social forays. If they went to a party and nursed their drink in a far corner of the room, all the while glaring suspiciously at the goings-on around them, they wonder why they didn't meet Mr. or Ms. Right that evening. Why were all those *other* people so unfriendly?

The answer, of course, is that closed and unapproachable people build moats around themselves, sometimes filled with invisible snapping crocodiles, that are felt by everyone but the builders. We've heard the following complaint countless times from such people after unsuccessful first dates: "Why didn't he or she like me? I didn't *do* anything!" That's exactly the problem: They didn't do anything to show their interest in the other person, or show any of their own tenderness or vulnerability. The tough part is that these closed-off people are usually not aware of their moats, or deny their existence.

Key questions to ask yourself in this regard include:

Do you think of yourself as a loner? If so, you may be walling yourself off from others in unconscious ways. Some self-identified loners are merely quiet and self-contained; others are aggressively antisocial. Naturally quiet types don't have to learn to be party animals, but they may have to give some attention to finding the right kind of social environment—poetry readings, discussion salons, small soirees organized by close friends—in which to meet people. Even then, they may have to work to overcome their natural shyness.

Anyone who is looking for a romantic partner while feeling openly antagonistic toward people in general is likely to place a terrible burden of expectation on prospects. Being expected to make up for the failings of the whole human race is a bit much. If you think of yourself as a loner, try to sort out whether your style is introspective or antagonistic. The former requires finding appropriate social environments and mustering a little bravery from time to time; the latter may require some deeper self-examination and attitudinal change.

Are you used to wearing a "business mask" or professional smile in your work? Again and again we find that busy, professional people who hardly have time to change clothes between leaving work and going out on dates often forget to change their style of relating between the two environments. For both genders, the damage to their openness and approachability is considerable. Many first dates are ruined by one or both people never getting out of the business mode (or away from business topics for discussion). Over the long term, professionals run the risk of forgetting that there is another, more natural way to relate to people they are meeting for the first time.

The best way to assess yourself on this issue is to determine how much time and attention your work demands of you. If you're spending more than forty hours a week at work, it's probably cutting into time you need for a healthy social life, exercise, and relaxation. If you can't find a couple of calming hours for "depressurization" before going out on most dates, you run the risk of taking your work along with you in your head—and then it's likely to show up in your frozen smile and controlled persona.

What do your friends think of your openness and approachability? This is a fair and pretty easy question to ask of your confidantes or peer consultant. You can also think back to how you met *them*; did you make and pursue the connections, or did they? Ask your friends if there's one major thing you could change to make yourself more approachable and responsive. You may be surprised to hear what they suggest.

Self-Assessment Factors:
Intelligence and Education

A warning for men on this factor: You're more likely to overestimate your intellect, and the significance of your educational record, than a woman is. Thus you're also more likely to use these factors inadvertently to distance yourself from a potential mate, when you think you are using them to impress her. Generally speaking, women will be more impressed over the long term by how you *use* your intelligence than they will be by hearing a recitation of your degrees and where you got them. Bragging on your smarts on a first date can be a total turn-off.

Red flags we watch out for in clients of either gender include demands that a prospective mate must have achieved a certain educational level, and mentions of membership in elite organizations such as Mensa. Generally we take these as signals of either insecurity or snobbery about intellectual prowess, rather than confidence or real capacity.

The best way to assess yourself on this factor is to draw up a "Self-Inventory for Intellectual Compatibility."

You can rate yourself as strong, average, or weak on the different *kinds* of intelligence listed below:

INTELLIGENCE:	STRONG	AVERAGE	WEAK
Rational/Analytical	_____	_____	_____
Mathematical	_____	_____	_____
Scholarly	_____	_____	_____
Intuitive	_____	_____	_____
Social	_____	_____	_____
Physical/Mechanical	_____	_____	_____
Artistic/Aesthetic	_____	_____	_____

Filling out this simple chart honestly may reveal to you that intelligence is a much more complex subject than we usually take it to be. That's why IQ scores are not reliable indicators of how people will respond to different kinds of challenges and environments.

For instance, a person with strong aesthetic intelligence may be able to arrange or decorate a room in a pleasing way that a mathematical genius could never manage. Someone with strong social intelligence may understand why a sensitive person can be hurt by a certain remark, whereas the analytical giant would only hear illogic in the same remark, failing to understand why anyone would react to it emotionally. A scholarly type may be able to memorize reams of information but have very little of an intuitive "sixth sense" to apply in decision making.

Rarely is any one person strong in all the types of intelligence listed for this self-inventory. Since our culture recognizes and rewards the first three kinds more than the others, we tend to assess intelligence in ourselves and others in a lopsided, unfair, or self-serving manner.

Understanding and appreciating the different kinds of intelligence is crucial to helping a relationship evolve in a healthy way. We call the above a self-inventory for intellectual *compatibility* because that's a more important factor between people than high test scores or degrees. For instance, in our own home John takes care of most of the budgeting and accounting because he has a mathematical bent. But if a lock on the door jams, he's helpless. Julie has the mechanical intelligence to get the screwdriver, take the lock apart, and find out what the problem is. Couples with complementary "intelligences" can help and support each other in countless ways, as long as they appreciate the value of every kind of intelligence.

If you really want to talk about your intelligence on your first date, it's wiser to discuss it in terms of comparative strengths and weaknesses. There's no harm in mentioning your degrees, honors, or achievements, if asked, but don't rely on them to characterize yourself. You want to prevent attitudes of competition or superiority from getting in the way of simple human contact.

Self-Assessment Factors:
Sense of Humor

There may be glum and dour couples out there living happily ever after, but it's our opinion that a broad-based sense of humor is a crucial quality for attracting people and maintaining a long-term relationship. By "broad-based," we mean the capacity to laugh at the widest possible range of things—from slapstick to high wit, from Marx Brothers movies to the everyday quirks and oddities of life. Having a good sense of humor about your own foibles and failings is a healthy attribute, too.

There are two problems with humor that we commonly see in people, and that you may want to question yourself about. One is sarcasm, the other is a tendency to turn everything into a joke. The latter problem most often crops up as a nervous way of making conversation in early dates; the former is more likely to be an ingrained, underlying attitude about relationships or the world at large.

Julie remembers going through a "sarcastic period" during her college days, when being sharp and caustic was a new form of humor to her. We've seen our two daughters go through similar stages. Unfortunately, we see too many people who have regressed to this collegiate kind of humor as a way of dismissing their unlucky dating experiences. These people often fail to realize that they're really expressing a lot of hardness and bitterness through jokes that are meant to "cut someone down to size," and that others may not find this predatory humor entertaining. It's more likely that people will find sarcasm distancing and cold.

Sarcasm or excessive joking can easily become defensive maneuvers for anyone who spends a lot of time in bars flirting with people who aren't interested in serious conversation or real relationship. To determine whether your sense of humor is defensive or friendly, think over these questions:

Do I tend to make jokes as a nervous habit when I'm uncomfortable speaking to someone? Has anyone ever told me that I joke too much? Do people ever seem hurt by my jokes? Am I more entertained by jokes with personal targets?

If any of these questions give you pause, you may want to reflect on whether you're using your humor to serve purposes other than those for which it's naturally intended: to appreciate and share with others your experience of everything that's absurd, unexpected, and paradoxical about being human.

Self-Assessment Factors: Patience and Empathy

More fledgling relationships fall victim to one or both partners' impatience and lack of empathy than to any other factors. We link these two qualities because they have so much to do with each other. Real empathy between people usually takes time to develop, and allowing enough time for that development requires patience. A common negative attitude that we see in busy, professional clients is that of "I need to move on if my new relationship doesn't seem to be working out soon." This attitude betrays an underlying selfishness, because such a person may be comparing a potential mate to a personal "want list" rather than waiting to see if a vital and perhaps unpredictable connection develops between them.

The person who is low on empathy may also be unnecessarily apprehensive about sudden changes in behavior on the part of someone they're just getting to know. Imagine, for instance, that a woman has had two enjoyable, exciting dates with a man who seems warm and considerate. But he shows up for their third date in a foul mood, seeming terribly brusque and insensitive. The woman has several ways she can react. She may think, "What a bastard! Now his true colors are showing." Or she may try to blame herself for her date's behavior: "What have I done wrong to make him treat me this way?" But an empathetic attitude will be both more objective and caring, leading the woman to ask something like, "What was your day like today?" If she has the patience not to jump to negative conclusions, she may discover that her companion is simply reacting to events in his life that have caused some short-term stress.

Thus, empathy is best seen not as an automatic, magical understanding of another's feelings, but *the willingness to gain understanding* by neither blaming nor taking on blame, and by taking the time to listen. That will always require patience. It may seem terribly obvious to say that people with these qualities have a better bonding potential than those who are pushy, impatient, and blaming, but the latter kind of people don't always know this!

One question can help you quickly assess your empathy and patience with others: *How much do you blame your past partners for your relationship difficulties or failures?* If it seems that others were always responsible and never yourself, then you probably have very little understanding of other people's struggles. If you blame yourself for everything, you're probably not seeing other people's flaws and problems clearly. When you can see that most relationship problems belong not to either individual, but to how both of them relate to each other, then you are most likely to have a fair and empathetic perception of yourself and others.

Can greater patience and empathy be developed in oneself? Absolutely. You can start to gain in empathy simply by looking back at your past relationships from your partners' points of view. The challenge is not to imagine what you would have done if you were in their shoes, but to try to imagine what the situation felt like *to them*, as the people they were, with their histories, shortcomings, and virtues. You can develop empathy in the present by asking partners, co-workers, friends, or family members in any situation, "How does this feel to you?" Holding off on your own assumptions and conclusions until you've thoroughly heard out another person *is* the learning of patience.

WHAT DO YOU REALLY NEED IN A MATE?

In this section, we'll look at five "desire assessment factors" that will help you compare what you *want* in a prospective mate to what you may really *need*. The better you know yourself, the less difference there will be between what you want and what you need. But so many people enter into the search for an intimate partner without questioning whether they have any such "conflict of interests" that it's worth taking some time to think the matter over. Again, the five factors that follow are by no means an exhaustive list. They do reflect the most common issues that our clients have discussed with us over the years.

These factors are:

> Physical attractiveness
> Honesty and integrity
> Femininity or masculinity
> Money, power, and accomplishment
> Religion and spirituality

Desire Assessment Factors:
Physical Attractiveness

We'll be saying "Don't pay too much attention to the physical" so many times in this book that we're not going to spend too much time on it here. Although we've noticed that women are becoming more particular about men's looks over the last few years, it's still chiefly men who tend to dismiss good prospective partners on the basis of looks alone, and who get themselves into unhealthy relationship patterns because of an addiction to certain body types or physical features (see the prologue to the next chapter for a case history).

In our matchmaking service we discourage the tendency to make snap judgments based on appearance alone by not furnishing clients with photos or videos of each other. However, we do provide a general physical description along with our personal opinion of each individual's attractiveness, in the way that a supportive mutual friend of two people about to go on a blind date would do. We think that anyone who might be judged not quite attractive enough solely on the basis of a picture deserves at least a first date to introduce all of himself or herself to another person.

The key to assessing your own attitude about this factor lies in understanding the limits of "attraction." The physical appeal of another person may very well be the first thing that *attracts* you, and that's a fine and healthy situation. But lasting relationships consist of a lot more than physical attraction! There also has to be mutual respect, shared interests, devotion, and determination. Despite some people's dogged and expensive attempts to combat aging, everyone's looks deteriorate over time, and thus maturity demands a growing appreciation for a partner's inner poise, grace, and dignity. If you're in your fifties and are still fixated on the physical flawlessness of twenty-year-olds, watch out. You may be trading in your relationship potential for a perpetual (and lonely) round of fantasies.

Desire Assessment Factors:
Honesty and Integrity

Here's the number-one concern of most of our women clients, and the factor that makes a screening service like ours worthwhile to them. Whatever the reasons, women are more often faced with deceptive dates than men are. Smart women have become wary of men who wind up their history of short, multiple relationships with the line, "I'm really tired of the single life." These men are likely to be faking the signals of readiness for commitment that women are looking for, in order to accelerate physical intimacy. The question that's uppermost in many women's minds when meeting a man for the first time is, "Can I trust what this guy's telling me?" When men bring up the integrity issue, they're more likely to express it in different terms, such as: "I want a woman who's happy with herself, who's not trying to be something she's not."

The problem with assessing integrity is that everyone believes they have it, be they priests, prostitutes, tycoons, or gangsters. Everyone has their own code of values to which they more or less adhere, even if those values amount to no more than "honor among thieves." So when we are told by women that they want a man to exhibit honesty and integrity, we usually ask them to be more specific. Questions we may ask them, and that you may find worth thinking over, include:

Do you believe in telling the truth at all costs, or would you lie to a date in order not to hurt his or her feelings? Imagine that you've met a man or woman you like on a first date, but he or she has no intention of seeing you again. Would you rather be told, "Sorry, this just didn't work out for me. So long," or "I had a nice time. I'll call you," or "I'm going to be awfully busy the next few weeks"? Where do *you* draw the line between politeness and outright deception? Some people can tolerate "little white lies" that others use to ease themselves out of an uncomfortable situation; some people cannot. It's important to know your own practical definition of honesty and be able to specify it in some detail, rather than just assuming that your idea of truthfulness is universal.

Are you upset by people who paint the best possible picture of themselves rather than telling the "naked truth"? A woman complains that a man who described himself as a "metals broker" turned out to have a job in scrap recycling. How would you judge that kind of self-description? Was it just a lie, an artful distortion, or a legitimate means of dignifying one's employment? This is one of those arenas where people will tend to make harsher judgments of others than of themselves, so it's important to take some time to think about this.

Do you distinguish personal integrity from professional integrity? That is, are there behaviors you might condone in business situations—like clever deceptions against a competitor, or manipulative advertising for your company's product—that you wouldn't permit or approve of in personal relationships? Would you refuse to date a convicted embezzler, yet think it's okay that all your home office supplies are permanently "borrowed" from work? This is a fascinating subject, because we've heard people react in so many different ways to similar provocations. One woman is horrified that a date brags about a shady business deal he's pursuing; another woman is impressed by a fellow who made millions in junk bonds. We're not saying that personal and professional integrity must be whole and synonymous. We are saying that you must have a clear idea about where you stand on such issues, and that you should think about how you actually *behave* compares with what you *believe*.

In all issues of integrity, the bigger the gap between your behaviors and beliefs, the more likely it is that you will make unrealistic moral demands of the people you meet, and the more likely it is that they will disappoint you. That's not to say that honest people never get ripped off. But we do believe that honest people who have deeply examined themselves on the issues of honesty and integrity are more alert to the subtle signals of dishonesty in others. The best way to avoid falling prey to the dark side of other people is to get acquainted with your own shadow.

Desire Assessment Factors: Femininity and Masculinity

Men look for softness, vulnerability, and gentleness in women because they experience these qualities least in themselves. Men look to tap into these feelings, just as women have traditionally wanted to connect with the strength, protection, and security that the masculinity of men offers them. To some extent, we think it will always be this way, although more and more people are realizing that they can develop all kinds of qualities within themselves. A man may never want to be as soft as a woman, but he can learn to be soft when it's called for—to soothe a small child's hurt, for instance. A woman may prefer to have a man in the house as a physical protector, but she can also learn a martial art that will provide her with confidence and security whenever she must be alone.

The old idea of gender roles and qualities was that a couple consisted of two halves that made a whole. Today's concept of relationship is that of two whole people who enjoy and appreciate each other's differences, and who can give something more to the world by being together than they could by living alone.

Everyone has to decide where they stand in relation to femininity and masculinity, what they are looking for and what they expect to find. As with most everything else, what really counts in this arena is openness. If a man falls in love with a woman who looks ravishing in an evening gown, will he be ready when she wants to become a week-end mountain climber? We have seen both women and men change in more astonishing ways than that. If you have very fixed ideas about how a man or woman should behave, you may be closing down opportunities for all the kinds of people you could possibly enjoy meeting and getting to know, regardless of their partnership potential. You may also be foreclosing on the growth potential of a committed relationship.

An important note: In a defensive mode, *everyone* begins to lose their sensitivity and approachability, and therefore their capacity to bond. We all bury our most desirable aspects when we are habitually afraid. We may think that developing a hard shell is part of becoming smarter, when in fact we need to become smarter while staying open. Male or female, people who can manage that are very intriguing. You know right away that you can't put one over on them, yet they remain friendly, approachable, and strongly centered in their femininity or masculinity.

Desire Assessment Factors: Money, Power, and Accomplishment

If women have an Achilles heel similar to men's fixation on physical attractiveness, this is it. Generally speaking, we find that it's older women who fall prey to focusing on this desire above all others, often because they are worried about their financial security as single women in the second half of life. Women who have previously been married to wealthy men have a particularly hard time breaking the habit. No one likes to sound like a gold digger, so we will often hear women who are on the lookout for wealthy men use coded language such as, "Money's not important to me, but there is a certain lifestyle I like to maintain." Or: "I'm really into the arts and I'd like my man to be a patron. It's just more fun to be in that kind of circle."

Another giveaway is a certain nonchalance about the advanced age of a prospective wealthy partner. "Age doesn't really matter to me," a woman in her early forties once told us. "It's more the vitality of the man."

John asked her, "Could he be seventy or seventy-five?"

"Well," she hesitated, "that would be okay if he's successful and really *vital*." Meaning: if he's rich enough.

Our advice to women of all ages: You're better off with a man who loves his middle-income work than a man who's miserable with his millions. Of course there's nothing wrong with expecting a mature man to have a reasonable degree of financial security and responsibility. But you should always be prepared to consider whether you would be happy with the same man if the two of you suffered a terrible financial reversal.

Our male clients rarely ask for women with more money, power, or accomplishment than themselves. Or perhaps it's that we don't cater to gigolos. We have seen a few reclusive men with considerable money or professional achievement who are fascinated by women in the limelight of politics or entertainment. Increasingly, men's problem with this factor is just the reverse: A fellow who's in corporate mid-management is unlikely to be open to dating a female CEO. We've heard men joke that they'd like to date a rich woman, but when actually given the opportunity they're likely to turn it down. In our culture at this time, it takes extraordinary self-assurance for most men to relate easily and fairly to women who are more successful professionally, unless their fields of endeavor are pretty wide apart and therefore difficult to compare.

For women, the salient question on this factor is: *What do you really want: intimacy or riches?* (If you can find both with one man, more power to you!) For men, the question is: *Would you be threatened by a woman's professional equality or superior achievement?* (If so, you may be nixing your chances to meet some very fascinating women.)

Desire Assessment Factors: Religion and Spirituality

One policy of ours may not endear us to religious devotees: We regularly turn down potential clients who specify that their mate much be of a particular religious persuasion. The reason is that such a requirement excessively constricts the field of viable candidates drawn from the general population. Another reason is that we feel such a specification is usually connected to a kind of closed-mindedness that goes beyond religious issues.

For instance, one time a young woman told us that she would be easy to match because she had only one condition for a potential husband: "He just has to be a Christian. That's all I'm concerned about."

John asked her, "Would it be all right if he has a few glasses of wine at the office Christmas party?"

"Well, no," she said stiffly. "I don't think that would be right."

"What if he swears a little when the lawn mower breaks down and he loses his temper?"

"Mr. Wingo," the woman replied sternly, "I said I wanted a *Christian* man."

It was clear to us that this particular woman thought of Christianity as a strict, unforgiving social and moral code that would be too demanding of the great majority of men. We advised her that she would do better searching for a mate at church functions or through the growing number of "Christian single" matchmaking services. We would give the same kind of advice to anyone who thinks they absolutely must have a Jewish, Muslim, Mormon, or Tibetan Buddhist mate.

We do recognize that spiritual growth and fulfillment are important to increasing numbers of people. But we feel that there are certain spiritual qualities that are common to all religious paths, such as humility, compassion, and wonder. Some people adopt particular religious beliefs as final "answers" to all the mysteries of life and creation. We think, however, that a person is more interesting to others when he or she can discuss the "big questions" in an open-minded, tolerant manner, while adhering to a personal moral code that keeps the judgment of others to a minimum.

In a sense, spirituality represents the sum total of a person's way of being. Any person who strives to make sense of things, to uncover a sense of wholeness within themselves that links together all the different parts of their lives, can be said to be living a spiritual life. If someone wants a "spiritual" partner, we think they need only look for someone who hasn't stopped learning and having a sense of excitement and awe about life on earth.

If you have a religious preference for a mate, ask yourself this question: *Does my religious preference narrow the kind of people I can meet, and the kind of ideas I could discuss with a potential partner?* If so, you may be limiting your choices not only for a mate, but for your own learning and spiritual growth. Better to keep your options—and your mind—open to greater possibilities.

ARE YOU CHANGING?

We hope that this chapter has caused you to stop and think—and feel—about yourself in some new ways. This may sound paradoxical, but one way that people limit their partnership possibilities is by deciding that they know exactly who they are and precisely what their mate must be like. This causes them to fixate on "wish lists" that a prospective partner must satisfy from A to Z . . . and guess what? No one does.

By honestly examining yourself and your desires on the factors that we've brought up in this chapter, you can increase your flexibility, tolerance, and curiosity about the people you will meet in the search for a lifetime mate. Although we sometimes stress the importance of self-confrontation on certain issues, it's just as important to treat yourself with a kind of forgiving attitude about what you perceive as your flaws, weaknesses, and insecurities. You must *know yourself*—and respect the person you are—before you can expect to meet someone who resonates with you in a healthy relationship. Time spent wisely in self-discovery means less time wasted and fewer wrong turns taken on the path leading to your partner.

4

Learning from Your Past: What Have You Been Doing Wrong—and Right?

Many a man has fallen in love with a girl in a light so dim he would not have chosen a suit by it.

—Maurice Chevalier

Sometimes we meet people who are so attractive, confident, and appealing that it's hard to understand why they're not already in the relationship they seek. Such was the case with Greg, a forty-year-old dentist from Dallas who impressed John in the first half hour of their meeting with his intelligent grasp of current politics and economics. Articulate and good-humored, Greg appeared to be in great shape; his physique confirmed his claim that he ran five miles every morning. With his ice-blue eyes, chiseled features, and a streak of natural gray through a full head of dark hair, Greg looked like a great catch for any woman in her thirties or early forties. So John was increasingly curious about what had brought Greg to a matchmaker.

"I think I'm ready for a change in my life," Greg said in a serious tone. "To tell the truth, I've been ready to settle

down for the last few years. I love kids and I want to get a family going. But I can't seem to find a relationship with any staying power."

"So I take it that your problem is not meeting enough women to choose from," John commented.

Greg blushed slightly, then smiled conspiratorially. "No, I guess I meet enough women. Maybe too many."

"What do you mean by that?"

Greg shifted awkwardly in his chair and looked almost penitent, as if he had something to confess. "Well, I've been in lots of relationships over the last ten years. But nothing's ever lasted more than nine or ten months. I seem to fall in love with these really great-looking girls and everything's fine for a few months, but then . . . After a while it just seems like there's nothing there. We run out of things to talk about, and I have to get out because I hate to hurt their feelings, you know?"

John nodded, already recognizing the outlines of a story that he had heard, with variations, from too many men. "Greg, do you mind my asking if these women are physically similar? Are you attracted to a certain kind of look?"

"Yeah, I guess so," Greg said matter-of-factly, followed by a boyish grin. "I go for a certain type, if that's what you mean. Most of the women I like are blonde, pretty thin, and have great figures. My last girlfriend Angela was a model."

Suddenly Greg was beaming like a twelve-year-old bragging about his model airplane collection. John was struck by the difference in maturity between the Greg who could discuss presidential politics and the Fed's policy on interest rates in a well-informed fashion, and the Greg who still looked at women through the eyes of a teenager. But "blonde-and-slen-der" might not really be Greg's primary discriminating fac-tor, John sensed—just the one Greg was aware of. The last girlfriend's occupation provided a clue about something most important.

"Most working models are not in your age category," John remarked. *"How old was Angela?"*

"Twenty-three."

"I see," John replied, pausing for effect. *"Have most of your girlfriends been that young?"*

"Well, no," Greg said defensively, then hesitated as if searching his mind for something very elusive. *"A few years ago, when I was thirty-seven, I went out for a year with Grace. She was thirty."*

"What did she do professionally?"

"Oh, she worked in this bar where I hung out after soft-ball league. We got along great for a while but then she seemed to get jealous about my success. After a while it became clear to me that she was really down on herself for not having a better education. But she's the one who kept dropping out of college. Also, she had a kid and a deadbeat ex, and that sit-uation really weighed her down. It just got to be more than I could handle. Besides, I wanted to start fresh with somebody. Maybe that's why I like younger women—no entanglements."

"Maybe," John allowed. *"But it seems that these young women have a hard time keeping up with you in other ways. Have you ever dated anyone with a serious, long-term profes-sional career?"*

Greg looked stumped. "Well, let me think. There was . . . no, I guess she was just a temp." Grinning like a young boy again, Greg looked ready to bail out of this particular challenge. "Does a pro lifeguard count?"

John tilted his head quizzically and smiled without replying.

"Oh, hell," Greg whined. "Where are the women who are beautiful and *smart?"*

John didn't say it out loud, but the answer to that question would have been, "Everywhere you're not looking." Greg thought he wanted beauty, smarts, and sophistication all rolled up into one female package. In fact, a beautiful woman who was also his intellectual or professional peer might have been too intimidating to him. By consistently selecting much younger women with less life experience and professional achievement, Greg was making sure that his girlfriends would never be threatening to him. He was also guaranteeing that he would get bored with them before very long.

When John questioned Greg about his family history, the roots of this pattern became clear. Greg had been raised since early adolescence by his mother, a powerful and independent woman who eventually became quite successful as an attorney. Greg was awed by his mother but had never felt much tenderness or acceptance from her. She was usually disapproving of his girlfriends.

Thus Greg's addiction to "blonde bombshells" served a couple of purposes for him, neither of them very constructive. By associating with women who were the polar opposite of his mother, he could get away from the experience of being intimidated by women—and he could irritate his mother at the same time. He was using his intimate relationships to feel more powerful with women, but this strategy wasn't helping him connect on a respectful and intimate basis. In all likeli-hood, Greg had separated from Grace the bartender not just because of her low self-esteem and "entanglements." It also sounded to John like Grace had come the closest to demanding an egalitarian relationship, and Greg found that too fright-ening to negotiate.

We couldn't untangle Greg's family history for him. He already had a counselor who was helping him work on that. The best we could do for Greg was to counter his habitual pattern of selecting relationship prospects.

After perusing our files, we settled on Pamela, a thirty-eight-year-old program manager of a public television station. Her education and professional status were comparable to Greg's, and we knew her to be bright, warm, and friendly. We also knew that she wasn't Greg's "type" physically; she was a brunette of average height and weight, certainly not as slender as most female lifeguards in their twenties. John pre-pared Greg for the shock by describing Pamela in terms he knew Greg would understand: "Look, I know you're used to dating nines and tens, and you'll probably regard Pam as about a seven on your scale for looks. But it's my guess that you need to meet a different kind of woman than you're used to. After all, you didn't come to us because you have a problem meeting women. You said you're ready for a change, right?"

Greg agreed, called Pamela and met her for coffee the next weekend. Afterward Pamela told Julie over the phone that although Greg seemed "a little distant," she found him interesting and attractive, and wouldn't mind seeing him again. But when John talked to Greg, there was a lot of dead air on the line. Greg grudgingly admitted that Pamela was smart and friendly, and that when they discovered they were both Southerners by birth, they found a few things to talk and laugh about in their shared heritage.

But Greg seemed reluctant to say anything too positive, finally blurting out, "John, I have to be straight with you. Pam's a very nice woman and I enjoyed talking to her. But the fact is that she's just not very attractive to me. I didn't feel any chemistry. I know she's close to my age, but she seems much older to me somehow. I'm just used to younger women in better shape, I guess."

Whenever we talk to clients who have shared a first date with mixed results, we have to make a judgment call: Should we counter their doubts and recommend another meeting, or agree that things just didn't work out and make new arrangements? In this case, John felt that Greg was still clinging to his old habits. If he wasn't pushed a little toward the change he'd said he wanted, his experiences with our prospects were sure to be unfruitful.

"If you're convinced this is hopeless," John said to Greg, "we'll let Pamela know and move on. But if I were you, I'd want to get my money's worth from our fee—which means committing some energy to work on a situation that's new for you. My personal recommendation is that you call Pamela again, and set up another date where you can do something fun together and then talk for another couple of hours. I think you're letting purely physical considerations get in the way of seeing this woman's lasting qualities, the kind of qualities that make for a good, long-term relationship. I know that you're not seeing everything you like on the outside, but maybe it's time to pay more attention to the inside. That

takes a little more time and attention. We'll do whatever you say, but I think Pamela deserves a second chance. What do you think?"

Greg hemmed and hawed for a little while but finally agreed to meet Pamela again on the basis that he "had nothing to lose." About a week later, he called John sounding like a different man. "I'm sure glad you pushed me into seeing this woman again," he reported. "We had such a great time the other night! I guess I wasn't very friendly at first, and when Pam asked me if something was wrong I just blurted out that she wasn't really my type. You know what she said?"

"No, what?" John replied.

"She said that was okay because I wasn't her type either!" Greg laughed and continued: "The funny thing is, that broke the ice for us and I felt like we could then talk about anything that came into our heads. It was as if I didn't have to keep sizing her up anymore. I felt we could just be friends without worrying about whether things were going to 'work out' in a big way. That's when we started to find out all the things we had in common, and the evening was gone before we knew it. We had to make another date just to finish our conversation! I don't know if this will go anywhere, John, but I'm glad that you made me take a second look."

RECOGNIZING UNPRODUCTIVE PATTERNS

Again and again we meet clients like Greg who are stuck in unproductive patterns of dating and relating yet keep hoping that the next person they meet will be "the one" who makes everything all right. Sometimes—rarely—that actually happens. What usually happens is that people stuck in unproductive patterns will fall in love with someone who *seems* like the answer to their prayers, only to watch their beloved gradually change in their eyes, eventually disappointing them in the same ways that earlier lovers have done. Then comes the cry, "You're just like all the rest!"

Anyone who's ever made such a complaint needs to take a good look in the mirror and say out loud, "*You're* still making the same old mistakes!" For the fact is that no person is "just like all the rest"; everyone is an individual, and deserves to be recognized and respected as such. When we're relating in unproductive patterns, however, we tend not to see people as whole and unique individuals. We pay attention to whatever we immediately like about someone—their looks, for instance—and don't pay attention to whatever we don't like. The tricky part is that our unproductive patterns are usually rooted in exactly the places where we're not paying attention at first.

Greg, for instance, thought that he was hooked on pretty young blondes for all the obvious reasons: their good looks, firm flesh, and youthful energy. But that was really the lesser part of his unproductive pattern. In fact, his chief (though unconscious) criterion was that his women not be as smart, mature, or accomplished as himself, so that he could always feel "one up" on them. This made him feel good for the early stages of relationship. Later on, of course, it would become clear that a lasting commitment couldn't be founded on such an unequal footing. Then Greg could decide that a woman just wasn't mature enough for him, maintaining his superior status even as he broke off the relationship. Then his roving eye would fall upon the next youthful beauty. It was a cycle with no future, and it was unfair to women.

CHANGING UNPRODUCTIVE PATTERNS

The inner workings of self-defeating patterns are always at least partially veiled to the people struggling with them. That's what makes them tough to recognize and change. We wish we had a way to undo unproductive patterns that worked for everyone, but neither we nor the best psychotherapists have a universal solution. In the limited time we have to advise individuals who are searching for a mate, we try to deal with each unique case appropriately. People sometimes find it useful to consult a psychological counselor for patterns that they're beginning to recognize but feel helpless to change. Sometimes looking into one's family history, as Greg did, is necessary. As we've suggested earlier, asking trusted friends or writing in a journal are other ways that you might be able to see yourself more clearly, and analyze your own unsuccessful patterns of relationship.

Following are a couple more stories of clients with unproductive patterns, and how we helped them confront and alter their habits. Although you may not share these individuals' particular problems, you may recognize something of your own struggles in theirs. We picked these two stories because they are similar to many that we've heard from clients. And sometimes the moral of a story is less instructive than the story itself!

She Told Too Much Too Soon

Sandra was a petite and attractive thirty-five-year-old teacher who bore a resemblance to the actress Holly Hunter. Sandra was painfully shy and self-critical. Our interview with her started very slowly because she seemed terribly embarrassed to discuss her relationship history. Acting as if she expected us to judge her harshly, she revealed in bit-by-bit fashion her unproductive pattern of relationships. She met men easily, tended to sleep with them almost right away, and couldn't seem to make any relationship last longer than three months. She told us that she understood some of the motivations behind her behavior; she had grown up with three brothers and a domineering father whom she had always tried, mostly unsuccessfully, to please. "I know I'm too obsequious," she confessed. "It's silly at my age to be afraid of every man's disapproval, but I can't seem to break the habit."

We asked Sandra how she talked about herself to men on a first date. What were the most important things she wanted men to know about her?

"Well, I try to be honest about my past," Sandra remarked. "Right away I usually let a guy know that although I'm really interested in a long-term relationship, I can't claim a lot of success in that area. I don't think it's fair to hide the truth."

We immediately pointed out to Sandra that this was not the way to put her best foot forward in a new relationship. By revealing her failures right off the bat, she was sending the implicit message, "If you don't like me it's okay because everybody else rejects me too." What she called "fairness" was really an expression of poor self-esteem, and a way to keep men at a familiar distance. Sandra was so afraid of being rejected by a man to whom she might grow close that she made sure she never got very close. But she would open the door to premature sexual relations to stave off *immediate* rejection. Behind this behavior lurked the attitude, "I'm lucky even to get a date, considering what a failure I am. If I can get the guy hooked sexually, maybe I'll have a chance with him."

Needless to say, this strategy never paid off. Men either took advantage of Sandra for a couple months, or backed away from her at high speed, sensing that her tales of romances gone wrong constituted a self-fulfilling prophecy. And they did.

Our advice to Sandra was simple: Stop talking about your past on first dates. We urged her to remind herself of her intelligence, her sharp wit, and her natural caring for others before she went out with somebody new, rather than preparing yet another retelling of her sad past. She could talk about her relationship history with a man later—and gradually, when the two of them had developed some trust, comfort, and intimacy. But why rush to establish a position of inferiority, and then try to compensate by offering herself sexually to men she hardly knew?

The other thing we did for Sandra was to counter her self-denigration by underadvertising the prospects we matched her with: "Well, this fellow may not really be good enough for you, Sandra, but maybe you should give him a try." This approach confronted Sandra's tendency to perceive all men as potentially harsh judges of her worth. It confused her in a good way, you might say. Her first few forays with a new perspective were rocky; for a while she kept bursting out with a confession of her failures on second dates, instead of the first. But late in the program she held her tongue long enough to connect with a very quiet, nonjudgmental guy and found her first long-term relationship in many years.

To be fair, we have to say that the tendency to talk too much about the past is usually more a male problem than a female one. Men will have a different motivation than Sandra's: Generally speaking, they are trying to resolve relationships they've left and are using women they've just met as counselors. Women often interpret this behavior as evidence that a man is still hooked on a past love, which is not always the case. Often he simply has no one else to help him figure out what happened in a relationship gone wrong. For either gender, we give the same advice we did to Sandra: Hold off on extensive revelation of your past until you have a good solid connection with someone based on your present-day experiences together. If you're driven by a need to confess and examine your past, take it to a therapist or a good friend.

He Oversold Himself

Danny, forty-five, was a red-headed, stocky, and strong fellow who worked in corporate sales—a job he admitted was several rungs below his potential, considering his intelligence and education. "I guess I'm hooked on sales," he told us. "I like the feeling of making a pitch and connecting with people on a daily basis. I tried a management position once, but it just got too lonely at the top, like they say."

Gregarious and funny, Danny was hard not to like when talking about anything besides himself. But in our interview, we were both a little irritated by his tendency toward self-promotion. He reminded us several times of the pedigree of his MBA, his numerous sales awards, and his role in clinching his fraternity's national rugby championship in college. After every boast he would look at us with a bright, expectant smile—as if he were waiting for us to pat him on the head and say, "Good boy, Danny!" His sketchy outline of his family history provided some clues about the roots of this personality trait: Raised by an insensitive father and a series of aunts, Danny had probably never experienced consistent approval and affection from stable parental figures. Hence his penchant for the daily positive feedback that a good salesman receives, and his tendency to oversell himself to strangers.

On the other hand, Danny was not particularly demanding in his requirements for a relationship prospect. He didn't judge women primarily by physical standards, and wasn't afraid of their intelligence or professional success matching his own. He even claimed to prefer maturity over youthfulness, making him matchable to a much broader range of our female clients than most men approaching middle age will consider. We were tempted to tell Danny to tone down his personal sales pitch before his first date in the program, but decided to let him wing it. Perhaps he treated attractive single women differently, we reasoned.

We were both right and wrong. Based on what Danny's first three prospects told us, he did treat them differently: He hit them with his sales pitch earlier, harder, and faster! We couldn't get much information from the first woman's feedback, beyond her remark that she found Danny "perfectly obnoxious." The second woman complained that he brought up his MBA as soon as they shook hands and sat down, and that the rest of his conversation focused on "me me me." There was no way she would want to see him again, she said.

Danny's third prospect was a little more kind, but still she gave up on him after two dates. "We'd agreed on a movie and a little snack for our second time out together," she reported to us, "but then he called me the afternoon of our date and told me to be ready for something special. Well, I didn't know exactly what that meant. He took me out to a very expensive restaurant, and I saw him slip a $20 bill to the maitre'd, who came over a little later and seemed to be pretending that he and Danny were old friends. The whole night went like that. At the end of it I just felt sorry for the guy. He seemed to be working so hard just to impress little old me!"

If something didn't change, it looked like Danny was going to run through his program in record time and never connect with anyone. John invited him back to the office, spread out his first three dates' feedback forms on the desk, and asked him to look them over and see if he found a pattern.

"I guess they just didn't like me," Danny said in an uncharacteristically downcast tone when he put the forms back on the desk.

"That's not exactly how it looks to me," John replied. "The last lady said she thought you were a bright and attractive guy, but you tried to control things too much. She couldn't get a word in edgewise, and she felt like you were trying to impress her instead of just getting to know each other."

Danny just shrugged his shoulders and looked helpless in reply.

"The message is, it's time to change your approach to meeting these women," John suggested. "I think you're smart enough to do that. What I want you to try is listening a little more, and fighting back that urge to impress. Two specifics I can suggest right off the bat, Danny. Don't talk about your degrees or your college days for at least the first hour of conversation, and whenever you get the urge to brag about something you've done, ask the woman something about herself instead. Then follow the conversation from there. Let her know you're interested in *her*, not just in making a sale!"

As Danny smiled hesitantly, John continued: "You're a very likable guy, Danny; you're just coming on too strong. Hold off a little, try to slow yourself down. Does that make sense?"

Danny agreed that it did, and the result was a near-miracle. His fourth prospect in the program, a successful M.D. in her late thirties, happened to be a vivacious woman who wasn't afraid of speaking up for herself. Since Danny made a real effort to hold himself back and listen better, her forthrightness helped the two of them set off some real sparks. Her report after their first date: "He was one of the most laid-back, easygoing guys I've ever met. At the same time, he has a lot of confidence. I'm very impressed!" For his part, Danny told us that he'd never felt so close to a woman on a first date. Perhaps that was because this date was the first one not monopolized by his sales pitch!

WHAT HAVE YOU BEEN DOING RIGHT?

While it's important to look for the negative beliefs and behaviors that may be behind unproductive patterns of dating and relating, examining your past experiences should be more than a fault-finding tour. Like Sandra, some people can become fixated on their failures while failing to learn anything from them. This generally means that they are not regarding themselves with any charity, not giving themselves any credit for what they may have been doing right in the past.

For instance, Sandra met men easily, managing to stay open and approachable despite many experiences of being used. Her availability went too far, of course, when she became prematurely sexually involved. But had she decided she was too friendly in general, she might have closed down emotionally in a way that would have only resulted in a different set of problems. We tried to help her appreciate and reinforce her openness—something she was doing right in meeting men—while learning to respect herself more overall. This is an example of what we've already said is so important for women today: Wising up is not the same as shutting down. You need to become smarter while staying open, and that calls for appreciating your positive qualities even in the face of unhappy relationship experiences.

What Danny was doing right was harboring few of the usual prejudices of men in the way he looked at women. He wasn't hooked on beauty, and he wasn't afraid of women's success or maturity. Beyond that, learning that he didn't have to "sell" himself to women really meant learning to accept that he was okay—that he didn't need to self-advertise because people naturally liked him (until he tried to *force* them to like him). What Danny was doing wrong was treating himself as a commodity; he did better whenever he could just be himself. This kind of situation occurs frequently with both women and men. Whenever we think we have to compensate for our flaws or failures, we may be covering up a lot of what's appealing about us.

The key to becoming more appealing to others, and more "bondable" with a potential mate, is to begin *changing* what you don't like about yourself, instead of just compensating or trying to cover it up. Changing oneself is not easy, of course; it requires a certain amount of confidence. The paradox is that you have to feel basically good about yourself in order to work on changing whatever you don't feel good about. Impossible? Not at all. The secret is in remembering to count your blessings from time to time. No one is in such bad shape that they can't uncover positive qualities and advantages within themselves that may have been forgotten as unsuccessful experiences in dating and relating seemed to pile up.

If you absolutely can't remember anything you've been doing right, and are convinced of your own worthlessness, you can at least congratulate yourself for having the courage to examine yourself. That puts you way ahead of many people in the social arena who blame anyone but themselves for their difficulties. After appreciating your own capacity for self-awareness, ask a friend or trusted colleague if he or she agrees with your negative self-assessment—after all, what have you got to lose? If a peer thinks better of you than you do of yourself, you should give serious thought to investigating this good news. False modesty is not nearly so appealing as many people think.

LOOKING BACK: QUESTIONS FOR REFLECTION

To help you develop a balanced perspective on what you've been doing wrong—and right—in dating and relating, we've devised a dozen questions for looking back on your experiences. This is not a test you can score high or low on, or that will definitely indicate your prospects for overcoming any lack of success in past relationships. Rather, these questions are meant to provoke you to question any automatic assumptions you may have made about yourself or other people, based solely on your limited experiences. (It's sometimes a shock for people to realize how little hard evidence is behind their certainty about "the way things are"!)

We're especially keen on helping you spot negative beliefs or behaviors that may be feeding unproductive patterns in your life, and on helping you proceed with a more open and positive mind-set after you've finished this book. These questions are not drawn from any psychological theory or sociological test. They're all based on our practical experience and insight as professional matchmakers.

You can write your answers in a journal, talk the questions over with a friend, or just pause to reflect on each one quietly. However you do it, take some "quality time" for this. If you have to put the book aside while you think about a particular question for a week, fine. Speed is not the measure of success in answering these questions; it's depth of reflection that counts.

1. What's the single most frustrating element of your unsuccessful experiences in dating and relating? Is there a "recurring theme"?

2. Is there something about "all men" or "all women" that really bothers you?

3. Is there any overt or subtle way in which *you* indulge in the kinds of behaviors that most bother you in the opposite sex?

4. Do you ever feel trapped by your own behavior patterns but feel that you "just can't help it"?

5. Can you find any connection between your chronic, unproductive patterns and important relationships in your family of origin?

6. Have you ever tried behaving oppositely to your chronic patterns, just to see what might happen? Can you imagine ways to do this?

7. What are the most positive aspects of your behavior in past intimate relationships?

8. Do you see yourself primarily as needing an intimate partner, or as having a lot to offer someone?

9. Do you think your expectations of a prospective partner are realistic? Do you take pride in having high standards, or in being open?

10. Would you rather date a number of people who might not meet all your standards, or "hold out" for someone who looks perfect?

11. Do you fall in love easily and have many experiences of heartbreak?—or do you have trouble connecting with anyone? Either way, can you imagine something you could try doing to reverse your pattern?

12. For the most part, do you think you are too trusting or too skeptical of other people? What could you do to strike a practical balance of trust and skepticism?

We're sorry that you won't find any pat answers to these tough questions anywhere in this book. These are the kinds of things you absolutely must figure out for yourself, that no matchmaker or even a therapist can resolve for you. People sometimes come to us with the expectation that we will not only find appropriate dates for them but magically rearrange all their relationship patterns as well. Frankly, that's beyond us. We do try to provoke our clients' habitual ways of thinking with questions like these—because the deeper they look into themselves, the firmer the foundation they will be able to build for a lasting relationship free of past, unproductive patterns.

LEAVING AN UNHEALTHY RELATIONSHIP

Mitchell was a fifty-two-year-old attorney who prided himself on his directness and his take-charge attitude. He often bragged about his ability to "tell it like it is" and "cut my losses" in his professional life, but he seldom took the time to reflect on why he found himself in so many conflicts that seemed to call forth those very capacities. A friend of ours, Samantha, had been living with Mitchell for a year when he came home one evening, announced that he had something to say, and brusquely told her that their relationship was at an end because he was "tired of taking all the responsibility" in their life together. "You never let me know what you want," he complained, "but then you act unhappy with every decision that I make. It's too much pressure on me, and I won't take it anymore."

Stunned, Samantha replied, "Honey, let's talk about

this. I know we've had our troubles recently, but that doesn't mean we have to call it all off, does it?"

"I'm sorry," Mitchell said curtly. "I've found an apartment and I'll send a mover tomorrow with a list of my things. You can keep anything you disagree about. But I refuse to get into any arguments. What's done is done." And with that, Mitchell was out the door.

Tearfully relating this story to us two weeks later, Samantha was still in shock over the cruelty of Mitchell's abrupt departure. "I guess he warned me, in a way," she reflected. "He always said that he would do anything to avoid a long, drawn-out ending to a relationship. And sure, we had some trouble communicating lately. But I had no idea he saw things that way overall. And he gave me no chance to respond!"

From what we could see, there had always been a lot of problems in the relationship between Samantha and Mitchell; her passivity and his assertiveness had always seemed too extreme to us. They were able to *lean* on each other for awhile, but neither *learned* very much from their opposite styles. Still, Mitchell left the relationship in the worst possible way—not only shutting Samantha out of the decision, but setting himself up for a repeat of his pattern in his next relationship. Whenever he felt too much emotional pressure, that would make him afraid of being discovered as weak and afraid inside. So his reaction would always be to resort to his "strength" by severing ties and forestalling any discussion. It was a sad way to live.

If people are sometimes a little irrational in their search for love, they can come completely unhinged while trying to make their way out of an unhealthy relationship. The kinds of promises and values that they would honor in almost any other kind of stressful situation can easily be forgotten whenever the struggle of separation deteriorates into a battle of opposing wills and hurt egos. The vengeance of hostile ex-lovers may make for titillating gossip, but it's healthy for no one (including the gossipers).

Occasionally we meet clients who confess that they are consulting a matchmaker because they are in the final stages of an unhealthy relationship. We usually take the presence of such a client in our office as proof that the existing relationship is terminal. But we do try to ascertain how much effort has gone into saving the existing relationship, and whether the prospective client has observed what we believe to be the basic principles for leaving a relationship honorably, considerately, and with as little long-term emotional damage as possible.

FIVE RULES FOR LEAVING

1. *Never make a final departure from a serious relationship without completing an agreed-upon trial separation.* Spending "time apart" before final separation serves at least two purposes. First, it permits both people to step back from the intense emotions of a conflicted relationship, putting all the circumstances in a more objective light. This enables them either to resume discussion of their problems in a calmer way—perhaps with the help of a third party—or to make sure their decision to break off is the right one. If that decision is confirmed, then the time spent apart becomes the "cushion" that eases two people toward the experience of living their lives separately forevermore.

2. *During a trial separation, make frequent assessments of*

how you are feeling. Virtually every separation will begin with pangs of withdrawal that must be allowed to subside before one can really know what life would be like without an erstwhile partner. (For this reason, trial separations should generally last more than a week or so—for most couples, we would recommend a minimum of one month.) As those pangs subside, one should look for certain signs of "healthy separation." Are you generally less depressed or anxious than you were during the relationship? Do you have more energy and zest for life? Do you feel "liberated" from restrictions and limitations that you resented during the relationship? Do you feel that you're able to begin learning and growing again? Apart from any simple lonesomeness you feel in being single, are you looking forward to meeting new people and adventuring forth into a new life? Strong positive responses to these questions will indicate that your trial separation should be made final.

3. *Accept your share of responsibility for your relationship's problems or failure.* It's best to begin this process during a trial separation, because it may help you knit things together again with someone you love. But even if you've separated for good, assessing your part in the decline of a relationship is crucial to learning from your mistakes and being able to move on without repeating them. How much responsibility should you feel? It's always safe to start with 50 percent, even if you're certain that you were the victim of another person. *Allowing* yourself to be victimized is your share of the trouble, in that case.

4. *After a trial separation has been made final, do not reverse the decision to terminate a relationship.* Hollywood loves "second chance" romances—and we admit that we have one!—but in most cases we've observed that they do not

work out very often for people past their twenties, particularly if a trial separation has been given a fair chance. When you are certain that the reasons to leave a relationship outweigh those to stay, it's time to go.

One warning: We will sometimes see people "stack the deck" against themselves while fashioning a pros-and-cons list about an unhealthy relationship they are trying to cling to. For instance, a woman once mentioned to us that her husband beat her, "but only about ten percent of the time. Ninety percent of the time, he doesn't!" It's also not unusual to hear people say things like, "Sure, she's still drinking after she promised to stop, but she needs me." Both of these are warning signs of codependent relationships, in which people make semiconscious bargains to support each other's immaturity.

From relationship counselors we've heard a good rule of thumb for ending a codependent relationship in which an addictive behavior is involved: "Three strikes and we're out." This means that if your partner promises to stop drinking, for instance, you give him or her two chances to fail before terminating the relationship. The first failure should occasion a warning that you are close to leaving; a second failure should occasion a trial separation. And a third failure means the end of the relationship, no ifs, ands, or buts. Anyone to whom this seems cruel is willing to let their partner keep choosing a destructive habit over their own health and the health of the relationship.

Depending on its intensity, physical violence should be tolerated even less. Shouting at each other in the context of a "fair fight" is one thing. Being beaten by someone with superior physical strength is another, and we think that the very first instance of that degree of violence should occasion a trial separation, if practically possible, and certainly the enlistment of professional counseling. In all cases, two strikes of endangering violence must be the end of a relationship. Putting up with anything more is a foolhardy exercise in mutual disrespect.

5. *After you have left an unhealthy relationship, assess and concentrate on its positive aspects. Whenever possible, look forward to the day you can resume a nonintimate friendship with a former lover.* The degree to which you can rehabilitate a failed intimate relationship into a respectful friendship is a measure of your character, open-heartedness, and willingness to get on with life. Carrying resentment about the past will certainly exert a drag on your capacity to form new and healthy relationships. We live in a time when many people experience relationships that begin with a not-so-successful intimacy and a more successful friendship thereafter, partially because too many people rush into sexual relationships before they are really prepared for that much intimacy. The less bitterness one feels about such a process, the healthier it is for everyone.

Of course, the aftermath of many broken marriages involves battles over alimony, division of property, custody of children, and child-care payments. Apart from the legal questions involved in any particular situation, striving for respectful friendship after a divorce is obviously a healthier basis for the continuing relationship than perpetuating strife that should have ended in court. Again, if you're more interested in battling your "ex" than in getting on with your life, you won't make a very appealing prospect to a new intimate partner.

5

Across a Crowded Room: Encounters of the First Kind

It's not the men in my life that count;
it's the life in my men.

—Mae West

There was something about William that made us nervous the moment he walked in the door. Slight and sandy-haired, pleasant-looking but far from striking, this twenty-nine-year-old accountant was personable and friendly enough. But he seemed unsure of almost every move he made. "I don't know if this is the right step for me," he confessed immediately upon taking a seat. His eyes darted around the room as if he were on the alert for unseen attackers, then he focused on Julie, certainly the most maternal and protective presence in the room. "But I'm not doing so well meeting women on my own," he continued, "so I guess I could use some advice and some better connections."

"That's what we're here for," Julie said softly, already alert to William's insecurity. "By the end of this appointment you should have a better idea about whether this is the right

thing for you. You can take the application and our personality tests home and think it over, and then let us know whether you want to proceed."

"Okay," replied William, "that sounds fair enough." *With that he clicked open his briefcase, removed a portable personal computer and placed it on his lap, then fed it a disk he had in his shirt pocket. In a few moments he was looking brightly at us with his hands poised over the keyboard. "Do you mind if I take notes?" he inquired. "I hate to lose track of important information."*

John smiled, suppressing a laugh, and said, "Sure. No problem."

After procuring some basic biographical information from William, we asked him to give us a little relationship history. Enthusiastically he launched into a rather detailed story about a girlfriend named Anna, mixing past and present tenses in a way that obscured when the relationship had taken place. He told us they had been engaged for a few months when she broke it off to marry someone else. Clearly William still had some feelings for this woman, but it was hard to tell how recently his heartbreak had occurred. When he said something about arguing with Anna at a football game, John stopped William and asked point-blank, "Exactly when did this argument happen?"

William froze like a deer in the headlights and broke his eye contact with John by switching his attention to Julie again. "Well, let's see. I guess that was the last game of the season in my senior year."

"Of college?" Julie asked gently.

"Yes."

"When did you graduate?" John inquired.

Gazing up at the ceiling, William said in a monotone, "That would be seven years ago."

An uncomfortable silence ensued, broken after a few moments by Julie asking, "Have you had any serious relationships since Anna, William?"

"Nope," he replied in a childish voice, then curiously dropped his eyes to his computer screen and typed for a few seconds. When he looked back up at Julie he said innocently, "Is that bad?"

Taken aback, Julie fumbled for words momentarily. "Well, of course not," she finally said reassuringly. "It's just a little unusual for someone your age."

"Well, I've been working really hard to establish myself the past few years," William said breezily. "I'm now a partner in a firm with a former professor of mine, and we're doing quite well. But I have to work night and day to keep it that way. That's one reason I'm here, I guess—I'm ready to find a serious relationship, but I don't have a lot of time to meet people. And the truth is that I don't do so well when left to my own devices."

"What do you mean by that?" asked Julie.

"Well . . . " William scanned the room fearfully again before sighing and slumping back in his chair. The computer almost slipped off his lap before he caught it. "Here's how it goes. Let's say I'm at a party and I look around the room for the most attractive, outgoing woman there—somebody who gets everybody's attention and looks like a lot of fun. I mean, I might as well go for the winners, right?"

John nodded and smiled gamely, silently noting the con-

trast between William's unspectacular presence and his lofty criteria for female companions. Then came the clincher:

"Of course, I know this kind of woman probably won't like me right away," William said matter-of-factly. "So I have to force myself to approach the woman I've got my eye on. Then, I don't know, I always get into these weird conversations where I can't really tell what's going on. Does she like me at all, or is she just being nice? Sometimes women seem kind of angry with me after only a couple minutes, or they act like they'd rather be someplace else. I just can't figure it out. Sometimes it just doesn't seem worth all the trouble trying to meet somebody."

Startled by the obviousness of the problem William was describing yet not understanding for himself, we exchanged glances with each other, trying to find a helpful response. John finally came up with something.

"William, what would you say is a fair assessment of what you have to offer a prospective female partner? You're an accountant. Give us the bottom line."

William smiled warmly, seeming at ease for the first time in the interview. "Oh, I'd say I'm an average-looking guy with a less than sparkling personality. I have a great career and a good financial future, but I work most of the time so I guess I don't have a lot of variety in my life."

"What are some of your interests besides work?" Julie asked.

"Oh, I don't know. I read a little fiction when I have the time, see a few movies. Not much, to tell the truth. I'm not exactly a Renaissance man, if that's what you want to know."

"So what you're saying is that you're a nice guy who works hard and is financially stable," John summarized. *"You don't think of yourself as a spectacular catch for a lady, but certainly not a loser either."*

William answered with a blizzard of keystrokes before looking up to say, *"Yeah, that sounds fair."*

Julie looked questioningly at John to ascertain where this line of questioning was going. Then John tipped his hand.

"What would you say, William, about the idea of approaching a woman at a party who's clearly not the most popular and attractive? What if you went up and talked to a woman who seemed more like yourself—nothing spectacular, you know, but nice, respectable, with average attractiveness?"

William frowned and looked confused for a moment, starting to attack the keyboard and then seeming to think better of it. *"I'm not sure what you mean,"* he murmured.

"Let me be frank," John answered. *"William, you may be coming on like a puppy dog to women who are all wrong for you. You could be shooting too high."*

Julie tilted her head and glared at John with her schoolteacher look while William's head dropped to avoid looking at either of us. John softened his tone a bit.

"What I mean is that you may be making it difficult, if not impossible, for yourself by approaching women whom you've already put on a pedestal, and then trying to have a casual conversation with them. When you say that you know a really glamorous woman won't like you right away, you're stacking the deck against yourself. You're admitting defeat and then guaranteeing it. I'll just bet that you open the con-

versation with some kind of silly or self-denigrating remark, and the lady can't figure out where you're coming from. Am I far off the mark?"

Now William was doing the glaring at John. "I don't know," he said testily. "Maybe."

Julie felt it was time to intervene. "William, I think what John's getting at is that you're not treating yourself fairly when you meet women. It sounds like Anna really hurt you and ever since then you just don't expect things to go well. So maybe you pick women to talk to who aren't likely to have a lot in common with you. That could certainly make your conversations with them very awkward, and your chances of ultimate success very low."

"Maybe I see what you're getting at," William said after a pause, then turned his attention to the computer for a full minute, typing away as if we weren't even in the room. In the meantime John gave Julie an "okay" sign to thank her for saving the situation. Eventually William looked up and asked, "So what do I do about it?"

That was a question with more than one answer, but the fact that William asked it made him a good prospect for matching, even if he was out of practice when it came to relationships. The first thing William needed to do was to start making better choices of women to meet, and that was something we could help him with. What he needed to do on his own, however, was to develop a kinder view of himself and a more realistic perception of his needs. Ever since being rejected by Anna, William had apparently adopted the idea that he must surely be inferior to women who attracted him, and that's why he came on to them as either falsely ingratiating or unpleasantly aggressive.

William also needed to shake off his past, and use the energy that was still attached to memories of Anna to create his future. And it would help if he developed more interests in life beyond his work. Every time we talked to William as his program got underway, we reminded him of these points, and were impressed by his willingness to learn. He benefited greatly from matchmaking simply because we chose the women for him to meet, and thus he didn't have to make a play for their attention in his usual unproductive ways.

Our first match for William didn't go anywhere, but the second proved more fortunate. Angela was a bubbly, self-effacing woman two years younger than William who had a tendency to make self-deprecating remarks and apologize frequently about her appearance, her intelligence, her education, and whatever else she felt insecure about at the moment. Without telling too much, we prepared William for Angela by suggesting that she might need some confidence-building— "She's much smarter and prettier than she thinks she is," *we told him.* "Don't let her get away with bad-mouthing herself." *We then told Angela basically the same thing about William.*

Because both these people were naturally attentive and caring, we thought that coaching them to counter each other's inferiority complexes might neutralize their usual tendencies to be distracted by their own anxieties when meeting someone. At any rate, something worked between the two of them because William reported back to us that they had a great time on their first meeting—although it ended in a mutual,

tongue-tied awkwardness. "I really wanted to see her again,"
he told us, "but I didn't know how to suggest anything with-
out sounding too aggressive, like you warned **me** *against. Fi-*
nally she asked me if I could help her run some errands next
weekend while her car is in the shop. I guess it's not very ro-
mantic, but I think we'll have fun seeing each other again.
Neither one of us knows how to do this right, so I guess we'll
just do the best we can!"

IS THERE A RIGHT WAY?

William's insecurity about doing things "right" brings
up a common misconception among single people in the
search for committed relationships: that everyone is playing
a "dating game" that you win if you play well and lose if
you're an amateur. Unfortunately, the dating pros out
there—mostly men—tend to be rascals and deceivers who
are more interested in making sexual conquests and building up their egos than in finding a lasting love. If you're
looking for warmth, dedication, and loyalty, then you must
approach every meeting with a prospective partner not as a
game in which you pretend to know all the moves, but as a
unique and brand-new meeting with another human
being—a meeting to which you ideally bring open-mind-
edness and a sensible balance of discretion and vulnerability. Of course it helps to have experience from which you've
gleaned some wisdom. But since you can never be fully prepared for what will happen next in the search for a romantic
partner, we think it's always best to think of oneself as an

amateur. (After all, the Latin root of the word *amateur* means "lover"!)

The tricky part is that everyone is *limited* by their experience at the same time they're *informed* by it. Particularly if we've had emotionally traumatic experiences in love, we may have learned some lessons that are not helpful or are just plain wrong. William, for instance, had mistakenly learned from his broken engagement in college that he was not worthy of women he wanted—a self-defeating attitude if ever there was one! He became so accustomed to this idea that he avoided serious relationships for years by becoming obsessed with work. When he did make occasional social forays, he inadvertently made sure that his clumsy approaches to women confirmed his negative self-estimate.

If you're serious about finding lifelong love, you don't really want to amass years and years of dating experience. But it can certainly be helpful to know something about the experiences of many other people over time. That's what we're going to give you in the rest of this chapter and the next one.

The rest of this chapter is composed of three main parts: a review of the existing ways to meet people, some tips on setting up a first date, and a questionnaire you can use to help you evaluate your first-date experiences. Then, Chapter 6 will take you from "dating to relating."

REVIEWING THE WAYS TO MEET PEOPLE

Print Personals

From their humble beginnings in the classified sections of alternative weekly papers in the early '70s, print personals have grown into a significant moneymaker for major periodicals, including the *Los Angeles Times*, the *Washington Post*, and some high-gloss magazines, as well as an industry in their own right. It's not unusual to find periodicals devoted entirely to personal ads and dating advice in major metropolitan areas, and most papers with personals now feature some kind of phone-matching service as well.

Regardless of relationship status, hardly anyone can resist the temptation to scan the personals from time to time, if only for entertainment purposes. And it's safe to say that there are more people who have placed or responded to personals than will admit it. Despite the increasing popularity and acceptance of personals, for many people there's still something faintly "trashy" about advertising your romantic interests in the newspaper right there beside the used-car ads and garage-sale notices.

We don't think there's anything unsavory about personals, but we have observed that many people launch their personal marketing campaigns without a good understanding of the advantages and limitations of this medium. Let's take a look at the major factors, both positive and negative.

Personals are an inexpensive form of mass networking. There's simply no cheaper way to advertise your romantic availability to thousands of people at once. If you write a good ad—or even a mediocre one, in many cases—you won't have any problem contacting people to meet. The question is whether you will contact the right *kind* of people. Answer: for the most part, probably not. You'll have to do a lot of wading-through and weeding-out of respondents, and that can take some patience. If you generally like to meet strangers and don't mind talking to a number of them who won't prove to be romantic prospects, then you may enjoy the personals experience.

Personals offer an opportunity to join the dating scene anonymously. Many of our clients have reported to us that they used personals to break out of self-imposed isolation after broken relationships or time periods when they had been working too hard to think about romance. Because such people are feeling a little too withdrawn to join clubs, go to social events, etc., they like the anonymity and control over responses that personals afford them. Thus, personals can be a fun and concrete way to go beyond merely thinking, "I'm going to get out there and meet somebody," and actually do something about it. Even when the ads don't pay off, the experience of placing them and dealing with the responses can create a greater sense of readiness for a next step.

Personals tell you next to nothing about what a person is really like. The downside of the anonymity of personals is that they seldom tell enough about you or anyone else to help you actually sort one prospect from another. Hardly anyone can write a personal with real objectivity; who wouldn't call themselves "attractive," no matter what they look like or how unfriendly they are in person? Also, the people behind personals often begin to sound alike. It seems like almost everyone enjoys romantic candlelit dinners, evenings by the fire, and walking on the beach. Conversely, a few people try so hard to distinguish themselves that they come off sounding more bizarre than interesting.

We think that the best way to counter the anonymity of personals is to respond to them by letter, and ask your respondents to write you a letter, before you meet in person. This is not a foolproof method, as not everyone likes to write letters or expresses themselves well that way. An alternative is to call respondents before you meet them, which is necessary in most cases to set up a meeting anyway. Use that call wisely; see if you can get a casual and enjoyable conversation going about current events, politics, or entertainment *before* you set up a meeting. If you can't, the likelihood is high that you have an incompatible prospect.

Our advice on personals: Use them as a learning experience. Even if it costs a little more to change your ad every couple weeks, keep revising what you publish in light of what you learn from your meetings with respondents. If looking for "tall, dark, and handsome" doesn't seem to be paying off for you, change it. Maybe "short, fair, and funny-looking" will help you meet someone more interesting (and humble!). Try to become increasingly specific within your word limit; instead of saying you like to go to the movies, list the last two that you really liked. Above all, keep a sense of humor about the enterprise. And don't keep it up beyond a few months if you're getting tired of meeting strangers.

Telephone Matching

Most of what we've said about personals applies here, although we think that telephone ads are one step up from print in allowing people to convey a bit more of themselves. Still, some disembodied voices can misrepresent their owners, in either of two ways. Natural-born actors may have an advantage in being able to create a compelling "performance" for their message that makes them sound more interesting than they really are. Conversely, someone who stumbles through a short monologue about themselves may be a perfectly good communicator in a two-way, intimate situation.

Our advice on telephone matching: It's worth writing a script for your phone ad that you try out on a trusted friend, and review and revise yourself. Keep it informal and friendly, but stay away from silliness or overtly seductive comments. Don't waste valuable time with obvious statements like "I'd really like to meet somebody special." Be as specific as possible about your interests and characteristics.

Video Dating

A demure woman client who had used a video-dating service before coming to see us related this misadventure: "I made what I thought was a nice, honest video of myself, wearing my prettiest long skirt and a red blazer and sitting outside by the lake, just talking to the camera about my hopes and feelings. After a couple weeks in the service, I had no replies to my video at all. I asked to see some of the other women's tapes, and I was shocked to see how many of them did their videos wearing bikinis or workout clothes, really making their physique the main subject! I thought, oh, *that's* why I'm not getting any calls."

More expensive than print or phone personals but considerably cheaper than most matchmakers, video dating sounds like a better idea than it works out to be in practice. It's true that you get a lot more information than in other media, but you can also get proportionately more deception. There's a temptation for people to act or make themselves look sexier than they really are in order to get the viewer's attention. Perhaps ten out of a hundred people will appear relaxed and genuine on a videotape, and some of them may only be good actors—that is, they are quite comfortable appearing to be anyone but themselves. And, like our quiet client, some of the most reserved yet truly wonderful people simply don't come across on TV. Overall, we think that videos play to our modern tendency to judge and quickly dismiss people based on their visual appearance and "performance" in artificial circumstances.

Our advice on video-dating services: Save your money.

Private Networking

In the simplest terms, networking means using your contacts to make other contacts that might be appropriate to your goals, whether those goals are finding a babysitter, a CEO, or a relationship partner. When you ask a friend if she knows a good shoe repairman, you're networking. Virtually all of us do it everyday without thinking about it, but a lot of people think twice about networking to find a mate. After all, the subject is considerably more sensitive than shoe repair, and you can't proceed as anonymously as you can with personals in the newspaper. Put the word out about your romantic availability to your gabby best friend, and soon the whole world will know, right? Not everyone wants that kind of attention. For those who don't mind, private networking offers the great advantage of being virtually cost-free, beyond the expense of phone calls and perhaps taking friends or business acquaintances out to lunch to pick their brains and address books.

The greatest difficulty with private networking is that it so often doesn't work. "I put my heart and soul into it for six months," one woman told Julie, "and I didn't even come close to meeting anyone appropriate." We think the reason for the frequent failure of networking is that most people don't know how to extend their contacts beyond the closest circles of friends, relatives, and co-workers. You may actually have greater success by tapping more casual or distant acquaintances: the gregarious sales rep who drops by the office every couple of months, the woman you had a nice conversation with at a friend's baby shower, the guy who spikes you from the other side of the volleyball net every Saturday afternoon.

Our advice on private networking: If you're in your forties or younger, try jumping ahead a half generation or more for networking contacts. Invite your boss to lunch and instead of hitting him up for a raise, query him about social contacts. People older than yourself are less likely to be in competition to meet people in your age bracket; they may also have a more mature outlook on good prospects for you, and have a more romantic perspective than your contemporaries. They're also more likely to be gratified that you've asked for their assistance on a personal matter. People in their fifties or sixties may also try jumping down the generational ladder, although they may find that younger people are too busy or self-absorbed to be very helpful.

Singles Clubs

Clients tell us that they have indeed met a lot of people in singles clubs. But they've ended up in our office because they haven't met a long-term romantic partner there. In fact, after their first couple of months of membership in a club, people are less and less likely to be dating anyone there. New members are regarded as fair game for dating, but after you've made three or four appearances you're likely to become "one of the gang" that sits around *talking* about dating and relationships. Also, the longer you go without finding at least a short-term relationship, the more likely it is that other people will vaguely assume there's something wrong with you. Finally, singles club meetings often become the venue for members' dates—that is, they bring people they're dating from outside the club to meet their old chums within it, and a fraternity atmosphere may arise, redolent of one's college days but not necessarily the best ambience for getting better acquainted with a serious relationship prospect.

Having said all that, we wouldn't discourage anyone from joining a singles club to improve their social life over-all. It just appears that singles clubs are better at making people busier, more socially active singles than at making them un-single.

Our advice on singles clubs: If you join for the purpose of extending your range of friends and acquaintances, you'll probably suffer less disappointment and enjoy yourself more than if you are focused on finding that special person in the club. Sometimes looking for a lover is like trying to focus your vision on a faint cluster of stars. Staring right at it makes the stars disappear; looking off just a little to the side actually improves your focus.

Singles Bars and Parties

If you like the kind of scene to be found at singles bars and parties, you can probably handle it all right. If you don't like that kind of scene, don't waste your time in one. The proportion of sharks and "dating pros" is higher in these environments than in any other, and there's a lot of game playing and deception going on. Plus, the more inebriated people become, the worse their judgment will be. The old cliché about waking up beside someone you met at a bar but whose name you can't recall (or never knew) is still played out by too many people; it's really not very much fun, and can be outright dangerous to your health.

Our advice on singles bars: If you're highly sociable (or just in that mood sometimes) and want to go to a bar with friends to have a good time, then there's no harm in talking to an interesting stranger that you meet while there. But if you do meet someone you'd like to see again, set up a second meeting in a nonalcoholic environment, following the guidelines offered later in this chapter (see "Arranging First Encounters").

Don't go to singles bars alone when you are lonely, depressed, or desperate for company. You're likely to set yourself up for an abusive experience—whether you're the victim or the perpetrator. Call a friend, counselor, or close family member first when you're feeling lonesome, and talk things out. A dependable rule of thumb to keep in mind is that you'll meet the right kind of people more easily when you go out into the world with a positive sense of what you have to offer, rather than a negative sense of how needy you are.

Professional Organizations

Like singles clubs, professional affinity organizations offer an opportunity for group networking. However, they're probably the least efficient avenue for seeking a mate. First of all, these organizations usually have agendas

129

that are not primarily social; you may meet someone interesting on a political action subcommittee, but that's not what it's there for. Second, people whose lives are centered around the same profession are often not interested in dating each other. Attorneys and physicians of both sexes frequently tell us that they *really* don't want to date their professional peers.

Our advice on professional organizations: Use your connections in a professional organization to network on your own time, away from group meetings. Call up a peer you've met and respect and ask, "So who do you know who's *not* a doctor?"

Sports, Hobby, and Special-Interest Groups

These kinds of affinity groups offer much better opportunities for meeting interesting prospects for relationships, for several reasons. For one thing, people are drawn together by interests that don't occupy them from nine to five every day. That means they are generally more relaxed at group meetings, and not anxious about shoring up their professional reputations or appearances. Plus, people from many walks of life may share the same off-hours avocation, be it chess, sailing, art, ethnic dancing, skating, computers, golf, or whatever. Talking about your common interests is a natural way to break the ice with attractive strangers, and team activities can literally throw people together in fun and exciting situations that dispense with the need for awkward introductions.

Our advice on special-interest groups: If you're not a member of any sports or hobby groups, try going along with a friend to one that interests you. This will give you an easy introduction to other members without the focus having to be on your singlehood, and it's much easier than walking in cold to a group where you know no one.

Professional Matchmakers

The first thing to find out about a matchmaker is whether he or she is indeed "professional," and the key question is: "How long have you been in business?" Almost anyone who throws a party where two people meet and pair off thinks they have what it takes to be a matchmaker. If you probe the experience of people new to the profession, you may find that it doesn't go much deeper than that last party. A good rule of thumb is to look for at least three years of experience as an established matchmaking service with good business credentials. Otherwise, you may do as well enlisting the aid of a busybody aunt!

The chief disadvantage of professional matchmaking is its expense; you can expect to pay $5,000 and up for good service from a reputable firm. What helps put this cost in perspective is the fact that a good matchmaker is screening a large number of people to come up with the most likely choices for you to meet. For instance, every person that a client of J. Wingo International (JWI) may meet through our service represents about ten people who were considered but weeded out as likely matches. Compare this time, trouble, and expense of meeting a hundred people at random to meeting ten people carefully chosen to have the best chance of "clicking" with you, and you can see the value of good matchmaking services.

However, it's important to understand what matchmakers can and cannot supply, for people often have unrealistic expectations. No matchmaker can guarantee that you will find a lifelong mate; the best any of us can do is to guarantee quality introductions based on careful and intuitive matching of people. You have to take it from there. Nor can matchmakers restore passion, openness, or enthusiasm to your search for love if you're not supplying these qualities yourself.

In fact, at JWI we regard it as our job to take the passion and emotionality *out* of the search for love. We objectify the process of seeking a mate for people who may be lacking sufficient objectivity, because they are driven by their passions or habits into personal isolation, unsuccessful encounters, and unhappy relationships. Matchmakers can help you open up your field of vision and increase your range of contacts, and they should help you balance the faculties of intellect and emotion in assessing your experiences.

Although you shouldn't expect any of us to be therapists, good matchmakers should be able to spot unproductive ideas and attitudes you have that may be blocking your search for love, and offer some pragmatic advice on changing them. In this respect, we sometimes have to bear the burden of being the messengers of unpleasant news. If someone is resentful about her chronic failures in love, she may well turn that resentment on us when her negative attitude continues to block the development of any relationships with matches that we've arranged for her.

Our advice on matchmakers: Above all, don't contract with a matchmaker unless you have a strong, positive gut feeling that a particular person is the right one to help you. Resist aggressive sales pitches, and get solid, informative answers to these questions before making a decision:

1. How customized is the matchmaker's service? Is this service just throwing together names that happen to be in the same file cabinet or computer, or is there some attempt to devise personality profiles of clients and match them both logically and intuitively? At JWI, we have clients fill out two standard personality tests plus our original "Profile Inventory" of qualities that clients see within themselves and wish to find in an ideal mate. We use a computer to do some initial screening of objective factors, but our final selection of prospects for clients is achieved by the two of us talking over our impressions and hunches about people. We're biased, of course, but we think that having a gender-balanced service vastly improves our chances of making good matches. You can expect to see more and more couples becoming involved in matchmaking, and we think that's a healthy trend.

2. Does the matchmaker run background checks (financial, criminal, marital, and employment) on their clients? JWI's standard policy is to run background checks on all male clients as soon as they join the program, and to run checks on female clients at the request of their male matches. This is an obvious reflection of the fact that honesty and integrity problems are more likely to crop up with men than women; that's just the way it is in our culture today. But all JWI clients sign a permission form to permit background checks when they join the program.

3. How "deep" is the matchmaker's pool of clients? A general guideline for a good service is 500 people of each gender. It's also important to ask how far outside the pool of fee-paying clients the matchmaker can reach to network for you. With our previous experience in corporate headhunting, JWI can tap networks of eligible singles well beyond those in our program. A matchmaker with solid experience in professional personnel searches will offer a real advantage to you.

4. Is any feedback, support, and advice offered on your dating experiences during your contracted program, or do you just meet one match after another without any additional input from the matchmaker? We furnish clients with feedback sheets to fill out and send us, if they wish, after every first date with a new prospect. We look them over and troubleshoot problems or questions that the client may have, and are thus sometimes able to "save" promising relationships that have gotten off to a rocky start.

ARRANGING FIRST ENCOUNTERS

Starting here and throughout the next chapter, we're going to give you lots of very specific advice about what to do and what not to do at different stages of a new relationship, from setting up the first date to deciding whether to turn a dating relationship into a committed one. We realize that not all of this advice will be appropriate for everyone. But we think it's best to cover all the bases and let people adopt or disagree with our advice according to their individual discretion.

As we've said before, we don't claim that our advice is based on psychological testing or any other scientific approach. It is drawn from our common sense and our experience of interviewing and coaching thousands of people on their relationship searches. So take that for what it's worth, but please don't mistake our guidelines for rules or our suggestions as commandments. Use our advice to develop and refine your own discretion—not as a substitute for it!

Let's assume, then, that you've made an interesting connection with someone and are about to set up a first date. What are some of the common-sense precautions and arrangements to observe?

1. *Arrange your own transportation to and from a first date.* We think it's important not to depend upon a stranger you're meeting for the first time for your transportation, no matter how well you may have hit it off in a prior phone conversation. Make sure that you can get to and away from the arranged meeting place under your own power. Should you decide to go elsewhere together (not really advisable the first time out), make arrangements to return to your home independently. Rarely should a woman allow a man she's meeting for the first time to pick her up at home— unless she's still living with her parents!

Arranging your own transportation also gives you better control over when a first date ends. There's nothing more awkward or boring than sitting through a six-hour conversation marathon with someone you'd really rather not spend so much time with simply because you are "captive" to his or her transportation. Being able to politely excuse yourself without asking for the favor of a ride home is an important part of social equality in the first-date situation.

Some people may also wonder who should call whom to set up a first date. A woman can always call first if she feels comfortable doing it, but experience with our clientele suggests that both sexes generally prefer for the man to initiate things. Anyone who accepts a call for a date should offer to split the evening's expenses down the middle. But if the caller insists on paying, you should gracefully accept the offer; next time you should buy the theater tickets or pay for the whole dinner, etc. You'll probably want to make such an offer late in the first date, however, so that you haven't obligated yourself to pay for the next time before you know whether you want it to happen!

2. *Keep it short, keep it early, keep it casual.* We hear of many first dates that "crash and burn" because one or both people load too many romantic expectations onto their first meeting. Ideally, we recommend meeting someone new on a weekend afternoon in a public place for coffee or a snack, having made it clear previously that you already have a dinner or evening engagement (whether you actually do or not). If you really hit it off and want to talk into the evening, then you can cancel or pretend to cancel that engagement. But in general it's wise to set a two- to three-hour limit on a first meeting, and never start later than seven p.m. If you meet someone for the first time for dinner at nine, there may be too many expectations raised about sexual intimacy that same night. Where you're going to have breakfast together is not the wisest choice of subject matter for a first date. Also, those who drink may be tempted to overdo it during the course of a long or late evening, due to their nervousness about the situation.

If you're a woman and the man seems to be pushing for a long or late-night first date, watch out. If he doesn't agree to your respectful request for an earlier meeting, he's probably not trustworthy.

3. *Give it more than five minutes.* Keeping it short does not mean automatically dismissing someone who walks in the door and looks less perfect than you imagined. Remember that you're meeting a whole human being with lots of

feelings and sensitivities, just like yourself. You're not there to make a hiring or firing decision and then move on to the next applicant.

Even if you immediately find someone unattractive and feel certain that he or she is not a prospect for you, show a basic consideration for that person's self-esteem and chat for at least an hour. Allow enough time to let mutual nervousness subside and a sense of casualness and good humor emerge. Who knows, you may find yourself making a new friend, even if your date is not particularly attractive to you. If not, you can then politely make it clear that you're simply not interested in talking further.

The only reason to clear out sooner is if the other person starts behaving in an abusive or overtly seductive way, and you sense danger. You may then want to voice your displeasure loudly enough for someone nearby to overhear, and then make sure that you are not being followed as you leave.

4. *Choose a meeting place that's somewhere in between noisy and intimate.* This is another safeguard for a first date, particularly important for women. A dark, quiet booth in a bar where people will seldom pass by is not an optimum meeting place. Neither is a noisy table at the fast-food court in a busy mall. You don't want to have to shout to make yourself heard, but you do want other people around—not just for safety reasons, but also to help give both of you things to talk about during the awkward moments of getting acquainted.

That's why a walk on a moderately busy public beach or in a safe, familiar park is a good first-date idea. This is what we call a "side-by-side" encounter that helps work off any nervous physical energy and keeps interesting things and people coming into your mutual view. Prolonged face-to-face encounters can be tense; they work better on later dates, when both of you are more relaxed and have established a comfortable pattern of conversation. Another advantage of having ample stimuli around you is that when neither of you have anything to say, time will go by much less awkwardly than if you are facing each other across a table.

5. *Try to be yourself.* This may seem like obvious advice, but for many people it's tougher than it sounds on a first date. "I told her I'd written a novel," one young man sheepishly confessed to us, "but it's only an unfinished short story. Why did I *do* that?" The answer is that even the normally honest person can get swept away by the desire to impress someone who seems interesting and exciting. Momentarily losing your head in this way is not a serious error; you can even make use of it to gauge how comfortable you feel with someone you've met when you correct yourself (more on that shortly).

A more serious mistake is to go into a first date with the deliberate intention to project a false impression of yourself. People most often do this out of a lack of self-confidence, believing that if they can "sell" a better image of themselves on a first date, then they can get someone to become emotionally or sexually involved with them before the image disintegrates and inevitable disappointment follows. There are three major problems with this approach. First, it's disrespectful to both people involved: The deceiver is not being fair to his own real worth, and he's setting up his date to feel uncertain, confused, and manipulated when she later discovers the deception. Second, people may simply see through the false picture that a deceiver presents, particularly in these days when everyone is increasingly wary about relationship prospects.

Finally, this tricky strategy is just not necessary for optimizing a positive contact with someone. People don't really get together because they *impress* each other so much; they gravitate toward intimacy because of intuitions and feelings that are hard to anticipate and "package" beforehand. You don't really know what a future partner will love you for, and you may fall in love with someone for different reasons than the ones you think you're looking for. So you might as well be yourself when you meet someone new. If you try to be someone else, you may be inadvertently concealing your most attractive features.

6. *Try to make a good impression.* Does this advice contradict what we just said? Not really. Making a good impression means presenting yourself as you really are in the best possible light. That means dressing well, but not so trendily that you'll be self-conscious, so expensively that you'll be uncomfortable, or so sexily that you'll give off signals you don't intend to fulfill. It means arriving at a first date as relaxed, alert, and on-time as you can manage, not rushing in late from work still mentally reviewing your to-do list. Above all, it means coming to a date ready to listen to and learn about another person, not to deliver a high-pressure sales pitch or pursue an agenda of sexual or emotional conquest.

Some people who concentrate *only* on being themselves without taking care about their presentation can run afoul of their own negativity and self-centeredness: "Well, I know I'm just a self-absorbed slob, so I might as well look and act like one." That's a sure-fire attitude for keeping first dates from generating second ones! The fact is that everyone experiences themselves in many different ways. The same person who feels like a self-absorbed slob sometimes may also know that she has a caring and neat self within her as well. Making a good impression can be seen as putting your best self in the limelight to meet someone new. There's nothing dishonest about that. And it may even lead you to realize that if you can put your best self forward for a date, you can put it forward at other times, more often than you're used to. After all, what's stopping you?

FIRST-DATE ASSESSMENT: HOW DID IT GO?

As we mentioned earlier, we invite our clients to send us feedback on their first dates. Then we help them troubleshoot any communication problems or decide whether to pursue relationships when there's any uncertainty. The following questions should help you generate and evaluate your own feedback, and give you a clearer sense of what you've experienced than you might have otherwise. Of course, some dates will give you a clear "go" or "no go" feeling. But sometimes even the most certain of conclusions can stand a little further examination, based on questions and factors that might not automatically occur to us from our own experience. Of course, many of these questions can be applied to second, third, and subsequent dates as well.

One suggestion: It's wise to exempt the first half hour of a first date from almost any kind of assessment. There's just too much nervousness and awkwardness involved in this kind of meeting to make a fair judgment about how the introductions go. Even "love at first sight" doesn't necessarily translate into instant scintillating conversation!

1. *After the first hour, did you feel mostly comfortable or strained with the other person?* If the awkwardness of introductions continues or gets worse over the next hour or so, this is a clear sign that the two of you are not "clicking" right off the bat. This doesn't mean the relationship can't possibly go anywhere, just that you haven't yet found a mutual language of connection. If so, don't make another date just to be nice. You should have a clear sense that you want to learn more about this person, regardless of the difficulties in communication the first time out.

2. *Did the conversation move reasonably well from topic to topic, or did you talk too much about anything in particular?* A danger signal on first dates is the monopolizing of conversation by either person or any one topic. In our culture, it's not unusual for a man to dominate a date with talk about his work, his problems, or an arcane scientific theory while the woman smiles and agrees with him. Then he may go home thinking, "What a wonderful gal!" while she stomps away thinking, "What an inconsiderate guy!" Of course, a similar scenario can happen with the genders reversed.

Either way, it's important to spot any serious imbalances in an initial talk and, if you can't do anything about it while you're there, try to sense afterward if the two of you could strike a better balance the next time. Remember, if you're the one who dominated, you may be a little less aware that there's any problem. Or if you felt prevented from saying your piece, you may need to be a little more assertive next time, and not just wait for the other person to allow you equal time.

3. *Would you feel comfortable correcting yourself or apologiz-*

ing to your date for any unintended goofs? Let's say that, when you reflect on a first date, you are worried that you talked too much about yourself or gave a wrong impression. Do you think you could call up the other person and ask how he or she saw it, or bring it up for discussion on the next date? If not, this means that you may not feel comfortable admitting any vulnerability with this particular person, and you should let bygones be bygones and move on.

4. *Were there too many inappropriate or aggressive innuendoes made?* Women particularly should watch out on first dates for men who say things like, "Boy, I haven't been out to Lake Tahoe for a while. Do you take many weekend getaways?" The most sensible response to such a precocious invitation is, "Sometimes"—as opposed to either "When do we leave?!" or "How dare you!" There's no need to presume the worst about someone who seems to be rushing things, because a lot of things can be said in the midst of nervousness and attraction that are a little off. But if you detect a pattern of aggression or sexual suggestiveness, from either gender, that doesn't decrease when you show signs of demurral, then watch out. A first date should serve a mutual agenda of getting acquainted and assessing the potential for further meetings—not either individual's agenda of controlling the situation, making a score, or proving one's attractiveness.

5. *Would you like to know more about the other person? Did he or she seem interested in seeing you again? Did you feel that the other person is open and touchable?* These questions provide you with several perspectives on the degree of magnetism the two of you generated on a date. If you feel there's more to know about the person you've met, if he or she gave you a positive message or signal about getting together again,

and if you can imagine physical closeness between you, then you should obviously proceed with further plans, if you haven't made them already. But let's say that you can answer the first question in the affirmative, but the second one you're not sure about. Then you're going to have to go out on a limb to ask for another date—or perhaps follow up the first one with a phone call—and sound out the other person on his or her feelings.

If you can answer the first two questions affirmatively but don't feel a strong physical potential with the person you've met, you may have a budding friendship on your hands. Sometimes physical attraction develops more slowly than other kinds of bonds; old chums do fall in love sometimes. But generally speaking, a total lack of physical attraction in a first date doesn't bode well for a developing relationship. For that matter, neither does the feeling of being "knocked over" by someone's looks, because that sensation may induce you to ignore other important factors about the person. As we've pointed out before, men will sometimes have to keep their fantasies about the physical perfection of a prospective mate in check just in order to see clearly the real woman in front of them. Judging someone according to wishful standards can get in the way of genuine physical magnetism that would be present otherwise.

In most cases, you'll know instinctively whether enough all-around magnetism is present to make a second date worthwhile, at least from your point of view. But if you find yourself in the position of asking for another meeting because there's some uncertainty present, be as diplomatic as possible to save both of you any unnecessary embarrassment. After a first date it's too early to ask, "Well, do you really like me?" or say, "I hope we can see a lot of each other from now on!" Stick to simple invitations: "I have two tickets to the play next week. Would you like to come with me?"

Even if you think the feelings developing between you could be very strong, it's best to leave both of you some room to breathe, back off slightly, peer at the situation from the sidelines, and do a little bobbing and weaving. If you demand certain signs of interest and emotional commitment before they've had a chance to develop naturally, you can scare off someone who might otherwise grow into a partnership with you. We've seen clients who decide they've fallen in love on a first date without bothering to ask the other person how he or she felt, and then blithely proceed to plan their lives together. By the time of a second date, the one in love may be light-years ahead emotionally of the one who's less certain, and the results can be disastrous. If you feel more comfortable fantasizing and strategizing about someone than actually calling him or her to check things out, you've probably not made as strong a connection as you believe.

6. *How did the last ten minutes go?* Like the first half hour, the last few minutes of a first date can be a little awkward, but we think this time period should be subject to careful assessment. Did your conversation wind down to a point where you had nothing to say to each other? The meaning of that situation is pretty obvious. If on the other hand you talked longer than you meant and were eager to keep going, then you probably have enough energy to carry you into a second encounter.

Unless the attraction on a first date is undeniably strong and mutual, we think it's best not to plan a second date at the end of a first one. It's better for one of you to say,

"This was lots of fun. Can I give you a call in the next couple days?" This gives both of you a chance to think things over, and not feel pushed into plans before you're really ready. This can be important whether you feel a mutual tidal wave of attraction or one of you is doubtful. In the latter case, a doubtful person can be embarrassed and intimidated by having to consider plans put to them at the end of a first date, when he or she might feel quite comfortable with a suggestion made in a phone call a few days later.

If you find yourself having to reject someone's overambitious plans, you can say something like, "I'd like a few days to decide about this. Can I call you?" or "I can't make plans without my calendar by my side. I'll give you a call." Such refusals should be accepted peacefully. Resistance, cajoling, or anger from the other person are danger signs of inflexibility; think twice about planning another date anytime.

On the other hand, when you suspect you're not going to be able to keep your hands off each other for very long, a little restraint, suspense, and delayed gratification can actually build the intensity of your attraction. It may even help the two of you look back later on the beginning of your relationship with a little less embarrassment. Then again, some passions are fated to start off fast. And we Wingos were never ones to get in the way of mad romance!

6

From Dating to Relating: Encounters of the Continuing Kind

She gave me a smile I could feel in my hip pocket.

—Raymond Chandler,
Farewell, My Lovely

When Julie met Hilary, she had two feelings right away: This woman would be easy to find a match for, and she was so charming that Julie hoped they could become friends themselves. A thirty-seven-year-old personnel director for a large media firm, Hilary was confident, articulate, and direct. The well-tailored gray business suit she wore to our office suggested a self-aware conservatism in her style. Nothing was overdone or false about her, but one got the feeling that she could "let go" a little more without running the risk of coming on too strong. Still, she had a good sense of humor and little hesitation about answering personal questions.

One insecurity that Hilary revealed early in the interview was her height. "I'm five-ten," she said almost apologetically, "and sometimes it's a real problem at work. I stand up to shake a man's hand when he comes in the office for an in-

terview, and if he's shorter than I am it's likely that he'll be on the defensive the whole time he's there."

Julie nodded sympathetically. An expectant moment passed in silence before Hilary hesitantly continued.

"What I'm trying to say is, I haven't been dating much the past few years—well, not at all really since my husband died and I started building my career. My question is, do you think I'm going to be at a big disadvantage in meeting men?"

"Oh, I wouldn't worry about that," Julie reassured Hilary. "It's true that some men are a little disconcerted by a taller date. But we'll check our files for six-footers for you. And if we find a good prospect who's shorter than you, we'll check with him beforehand. I don't think you'll have to deal with any awkwardness over your height."

Hilary seemed relieved, and relaxed a little more into her chair. Julie was curious about Hilary's emotional history, and tried to find the right words to inquire diplomatically.

"If you don't mind my asking, Hilary, what was your husband like? Did you have a good marriage?"

Hilary's expression turned a little wistful as she tilted her head and pulled at one of her earrings. "Oh, yes, very good. I couldn't have asked for better at the time, I think. I met Stoddard in college. He was one of my professors, in fact, although we didn't start dating until after I had graduated and was working on campus. Anyway, he was fifteen years older and much more worldly than I when we met. I guess I was under his wing for some time, although he was very liberal-minded—more so than I, if you want to know the truth. He really pushed me to develop myself and become as self-

reliant as possible. I thank him every day for that, now that he's gone."

"There must have been a big change in your life when he passed away," Julie remarked gently.

"You can say that again," Hilary replied. "Stoddard's heart attack was completely unexpected. We'd only been married a few years, and while we'd taken care of some contingencies together, I just wasn't prepared for his being out of the picture all of a sudden. There I was, a secretary in university administration taking some graduate business courses, but I had absolutely no strategy for building a career that might go somewhere. When I got my head together a few months after Stoddard's death, I decided I wasn't likely to remarry soon. That was seven years ago. So I just threw myself into getting my master's degree and hunting this job. I guess I'm a real career woman now. I'm certainly a different person than when I was the young wife of a professor. "

Now Julie began to understand some of her natural connection with Hilary; after all, Julie married a professor herself while starting out on her first career in education. She could imagine the shock of losing a lifemate near the beginning of building a life together, and was impressed by Hilary's evident growth and self-confidence. And Julie was curious about the change of direction that Hilary had evidently chosen by coming to see a matchmaker.

"So where are you now, Hilary?" Julie inquired. "What made you decide to look for a new partner?"

"Oh, lots of things I guess," Hilary said thoughtfully. "I'm getting older, and my career is pretty stable right now. I'm more organized than I used to be, and I find more time on

my hands than I know what to do with alone. I guess it's just time to expand my life beyond work. I think I have a lot more than that to give."

"Do you still miss Stoddard?" asked Julie.

"Not in a constant way. I get a little sad on certain holidays and our anniversaries, you know. But as I said, I'm a different person than the woman who married Stoddard. It's almost like another lifetime when I look back on it."

"The reason I ask," Julie commented, "is that we need to make sure you're not looking for someone just like your husband. It just wouldn't be fair to us or yourself if you signed on to the program with that kind of expectation."

Hilary smiled warmly. "No problem. I understand what you mean, and you don't have to worry. The truth is, I really don't need a man like Stoddard now. He was a little bit of a father to me, and there was nothing wrong with that at the time. But I've grown up in some of the ways that he always encouraged me to. So I guess I'm interested in a more equal partnership than my marriage was."

"What else are you looking for in a new husband?"

Hilary laughed abruptly, and flushed slightly red. "I'm sorry, it's not what you said that's funny, it's that I suddenly saw myself in a new car lot, looking at sticker tags." Hilary pressed three fingers to her lips momentarily, evidently suppressing another laugh. "I guess I just feel a little awkward about all this."

"That's all right," Julie reassured her. "Almost everyone does. Let me ask a little bit easier question. Since you meet a lot of people in your line of work, why did you decide to consult with us?"

"That one's easy. Most of the men I interview for the company are at least five years younger than I, and they're looking for entry or mid-management positions. I can't date anyone I hire, and the rest, well, I just don't think they'd respond to any overtures, if you know what I mean. Though I have to admit that I've met some cuties over the last few years." Hilary arched her eyebrows, getting a laugh out of Julie, and then continued: "I really need to network outside my usual connections, that's all. And after all these years, I'm not so good at flirting in bars. Frankly, I can't even imagine it!"

Julie assured Hilary that she understood her reluctance on that score, and the interview continued for another hour or so, Julie feeling increasingly impressed by Hilary's charm and evident readiness to pursue a new phase in her life. This was a case where we didn't even have to run a computer scan to come up with a first prospect. Julie knew before the interview was over that she wanted to try a meeting between Hilary and Perry, a 6'2", forty-two-year-old attorney who had no fear of accomplished and independent women. Perry was something of a renaissance man, with interests and involvements ranging far beyond his profession, who could probably match Hilary's late husband for worldliness and intelligence. Like Hilary, Perry was also warm and outgoing. Julie was excited that she had a match made in heaven this time. After giving them both the necessary information about each other, she noted the date that Perry said he would call Hilary, and waited impatiently to hear what happened next.

After two weeks without a call or a feedback from either of them, Julie couldn't stand the suspense anymore and called Perry to see how things had gone on his first date with Hilary. Surprisingly, his reply was hesitant and strained.

"Well, Julie . . . to tell the truth, I guess I was just going to let this one slide on by. I don't think I'd care to see her again. Don't get me wrong—I think she's a classy and attractive lady. Very mature, but a little cool and distant."

"Really?" said Julie, stunned.

"Yes, I'm afraid so," Perry continued. "She seemed to alternate between being completely aloof whenever I asked her a question, and then grilling me on my past, my likes and dislikes, and my future plans. I felt like I was being interviewed for some kind of position, instead of having a friendly get-acquainted meeting."

Uh-oh, *Julie thought to herself silently, already suspecting what might have gone wrong on this date. Still convinced that the match was workable, Julie tried to make a save.*

"Perry, would you mind if I called Hilary and gave her some of your feedback? The reason I ask is that she and I had such a delightful talk together, but I think she might have frozen up a little with you. She's been out of the social scene for a while, you know. If there was any chance of you meeting her again, I just have the feeling that you might see a different person."

"Well, if you say so," Perry replied. It was a good sign that he relented easily, Julie thought. "But make it clear that I wouldn't ever want to hurt Hilary's feelings, okay?" Perry asked. "It was just an odd meeting; things didn't feel quite right."

"I understand," said Julie. "That kind of thing hap-

pens all the time. But maybe I can help smooth out some of the rough spots between you two, because I think you're both wonderful people who might enjoy getting to know each other better."

"All right," chuckled Perry. "You might be right. I'll keep my options open."

When Julie called Hilary, she was only halfway through Perry's review of the date before Hilary interrupted in a self-chastising tone. "You don't have to say anymore, Julie. I know I blew it. In fact, I went home after seeing Perry and stomped around the house saying, 'I blew it! I blew it!' I'd just had a bad day at work, and I got off late, and I was pretty nervous on top of that. I think I went on automatic and treated Perry just like I would have a job applicant— even worse, probably. Poor guy, I guess he really did feel like I was grilling him. And too bad—I really thought he was nice, and pretty handsome too. Oh well . . . you win some, you lose some, I guess."

Julie listened patiently to Hilary's confession until she could get a word in edgewise. "Well, all might not be lost, Hilary," she suggested. "Perry seemed very concerned that his feedback shouldn't hurt your feelings, and that's a good sign that you two might still have some potential. Would you feel okay about my calling him back and explaining that you were a little nervous, that you didn't show your best side, and that you would like to give it another try? I can't say for sure, but my gut feeling is that he'd go for it."

"Oh, could you really do that, Julie?" Hilary said with real excitement in her voice. "That would be wonderful. There's a company picnic coming up that I'd really like to

153

have a date for—especially a date like him! I think I'd be a lot more relaxed on a Saturday afternoon in the park than I was on that awful Friday night. Anyway, I couldn't do any worse than I have already."

"Fine," said Julie. "Let me give him a call and see what he says. If he says no, I'll call you back again. But I'll just bet you'll be hearing from Perry again next. Is that all right with you?"

"Absolutely," replied Hilary. "That would be just great, as a matter of fact."

As it turned out, Perry did go along with Julie's save, and he and Hilary dated four or five times more over the next few months. Eventually each of them went on to other, more serious romances, but they've remained friends ever since. Julie's match turned out not to be "made in heaven" after all, but she did help two good people see beyond their crossed signals and initial awkwardness to make a genuine, enjoyable connection.

In the matchmaking business, we call that a success, regardless of how far it goes. We frequently remind our clients that the search for a mate is not a win/lose contest or a treasure hunt, but an important part of their own growth process. As they learn better how to present themselves honestly and get a clearer picture of how others see them, they can turn more of their own initial awkward encounters into second chances for love and friendship.

SIGNALS FOR SINGLES

When you're ambivalent about dating for any reason, you're likely to give off signals about your availability and interest that are the opposite of what you intend. In Hilary's case, she appeared cold and unfriendly on her first date with Perry not just because she was nervous and distracted, but also because she was naturally uncertain about starting off on a search for a new mate after so many years alone. Unused to meeting men in this context, what felt instinctively safest to Hilary was to continue her professional behavior on her date, and so that's what she did. Although she didn't say so, it's safe to assume that when she got home from the date realizing she'd blown it, she actually felt halfway relieved—for a little while. But by the next day she probably realized that it was counterproductive to shield herself so effectively from exactly the kind of personal connection she meant to be looking for!

This kind of problem is the chief reason that we offer clients the opportunity to send us feedback on their first dates. We also offer advice and sometimes intervention to smooth out communication difficulties between people who felt some mutual attraction, but simply didn't connect very well the first time out. To do this kind of service for yourself, the first step is to assess a difficult date using the questions we offered at the end of the last chapter. Assuming that you're interested in seeing the other person again, then you'll have to muster the courage to call her or him and say something like, "I know that things seemed a little awkward between us the other night, but I want you to know that I found you interesting and attractive. If I gave off any mixed signals, I'd like to have another chance to explain myself a little better."

One warning: Don't ever apologize or explain too much before you've heard the other person's opinion about how things went. If you tend toward a lot of self-criticism, you may have perceived that a date was more problematic than it seemed to the other person. On the other hand, if you felt a first date was wonderful and then encounter reluctance from the other person while you're offering a second meeting, first check out the signals you gave. You can do this diplomatically by asking, "Was there anything I did to make you uncomfortable? I had a really good time, so I hope I didn't come on too strong for you. Can we talk about this over coffee soon, or do you need some time to think it over?"

In these days when so many people are carrying around hurts and suspicion based on bitter relationship experiences, letting someone know that you're always open to giving things a little more time is one of the best signals you can give. Professional women and men can become so accustomed to meeting deadlines and production quotas at work that they may try to put the development of intimacy on a timeline, too—and then turn away from a potentially rewarding relationship just because it seems to be behind schedule. Men are particularly prone to this error in regard to sexual intimacy. From women we've heard many stories of men saying something like this on an early date: "Sex is very important to me, so I need to know how ready and willing you are. We don't have to do it right away, but I do need to know that it will be soon—okay?"

In our opinion, any woman who's offended or intimidated by this aggressive signal should say, "Sex is very important to me too, and that's why I need some time to see how our relationship develops before I can say when I'm ready. Okay?" If a guy likes you and is talking to you for the right reasons, he will give you the time you request. If he signals a lot of anger or petulance, then he's probably not a good prospect for a mature relationship. We'll have more to say about this in the "Sexual Timing" section later in this chapter.

OLD-FASHIONED FLIRTING

Besides patience, another common casualty of our accelerated, results-oriented lifestyles is the art of old-fashioned flirting. Some people have become so businesslike and self-defensive that they have no time or tolerance for the subtle but exciting signals of interest that constitute flirtation: the lingering gaze into another's eyes; the light but electrifying touch of a hand on another's arm or shoulder; the unexpected favor, courtesy, or treat that might mean only friendliness, or that might suggest a little more.

We would be remiss if we didn't acknowledge that another enemy of old-fashioned flirting is the recently acknowledged epidemic of sexual harassment, especially in the workplace. Whether one is afraid of becoming a victim or being seen as a perpetrator of sexual harassment, the contemporary anxiety over this issue tends to make everyone back away from flirting, and we think that's too bad. While there's no way to take all the danger and uncertainty out of sexuality, we think there are a few reliable guidelines for discerning harassment from flirtation:

Flirtation is subtle. The tantalizing thing about flirtation is that you're not quite sure when you've been flirted with, at least in the early stages of a developing relationship. Its message is light: "I'm playing with you in a friendly way because I'd like to get to know you better." By contrast, most sexual harassment soon becomes overt. Its message is generally coarse, crude, and predatory.

Flirtation makes you feel good. The worst feeling that true flirtation should ever give you is one of suspense. At best, flirting makes you feel excited and admired on the receiving end, and excited and hopeful on the giving end. But harassment generally inspires anger and a sense of being demeaned. If you think you are only flirting but encounter angry reactions from another person, stop what you're doing immediately. Either you're actually committing harassment, or the other person is not receptive to flirtation at the moment. Anyone who continues with suggestive behavior after being asked to stop is indeed committing sexual or emotional harassment. That's a failsafe guideline.

Flirtation is creative and unpredictable. Because sincere flirtation really is an attempt to accelerate the process of getting to know each other, it changes from one incident to the next. People who like each other actually learn a lot through their flirting, and so they get better at doing it in an increasingly personalized way. Harassment tends to fall into a pattern of repetitive behaviors, in which one person is suggesting or doing something again and again to the other without ever getting or accepting the message that it's unpleasant and unwanted. In fact, harassment may intensify when it's resisted; but what's growing between the two people involved is ill will, not intimacy. If you find yourself the subject of intensifying harassment, blow the whistle.

It's impossible for us to provide precise guidelines about when, how much, and what kind of flirting may be appropriate for every kind of situation. What we can say is that despite all the barriers, anxieties, and confusion of the modern social scene, flirting still comes naturally to people with a strong attraction to each other. If you've checked out your motivations and you're reasonably certain that the recipient of your attention is not being offended by your playful attention, then you can let nature take its course.

FOUR CHECK-OFFS FOR A DEVELOPING RELATIONSHIP

In this section and the next, we're going to give you two different ways to assess how a relationship is going and whether you should continue to pursue it toward intimacy and commitment. Both kinds of assessment can start with date number one. But you may find that the "four check-offs" we're about to offer will apply best to the first four or five dates. The Wingo 51-80 Principle, explained in the next section, will also provide guidance beyond that stage, right up to the decision for long-term commitment.

We should stress that none of these ideas are rules that can be rigidly applied to everyone and every kind of relationship. Rather, they are guidelines for anyone who is uncertain about where a relationship is going. They can also help anyone who's pretty certain about their relationship check out some factors that they may not be considering at the moment, but that can become very important at a later time. We regularly recommend both kinds of assessment to our clients who have met good prospects through the JWI program.

If you've had a first date with someone whom you're

considering seeing again, here are four important check-offs to keep in mind:

✓ *Does time pass quickly in the other person's presence?* This factor is impossible to analyze logically, but it's crucial to long-term compatibility. When you really hit if off with someone, you can spend hours in conversation without noticing where the time has gone. A desire to learn as much as possible about each other becomes your mutual first priority, and that positive energy will tend to organize things for the two of you, rapidly decreasing the awkwardness of making plans and taking next steps together. You shouldn't look for this kind of rapport too early; it's to be assumed that your first and second dates will occur in pretty artificial circumstances where a certain amount of hard introductory data has to be exchanged to establish feelings of comfort and safety, and to satisfy curiosity.

But if you're on a third or fourth date with someone and find that you're looking at your watch a lot, or looking forward to being by yourself soon, then you may want to question why you're pursuing this relationship. Some people have become so jaundiced in their search for love that they've given up on finding magic, and are willing to settle for someone who seems "nice" or seems likely to deliver certain desired factors: money, sex, security, prestige. Beware this sense of "biding your time" to get what you want from someone. You might be waiting for the rest of your life for what you really need.

✓ *Do the two of you laugh together?* It's our opinion that a lighthearted sense of enjoying life together is essential to forming a committed, healthy relationship. That's not to say that people who are negative, glum, and frequently angry with each other never stay together—who doesn't know such a couple with a long track record? But when it comes to choosing a glue for lifelong attachments, we fervently recommend the kind that's based on joy, a shared sense of fun, and a mutual capacity to laugh at oneself.

Notice also that we said "laugh together" in this check-off. Becoming the object of another person's ridicule or the passive audience of someone's ongoing comedy routine is not the same as having a merry old time together. While people's ability to make jokes or come up with wry observations on life are seldom equally matched, it is important to respect each other's sense of humor as is. One partner may have a bizarre outlook on life while the other is dry and subtle. The question is not whether one style is funnier than the other, but whether you seem funny to each other. If so, you've got a precious advantage in making a life together.

✓ *Do you usually come away from talking to the other person with stimulating information and insights?* This is a key factor for determining whether you're really making a connection with someone, or just wishing or pretending that you are. We've had clients who have met someone who fascinated them in some way—due to physical attraction, status, or financial clout—but with whom they simply weren't compatible. Sometimes a powerful fascination can make a person want to create a relationship where there's really no potential for one, and so they will put up with a lot of mixed feelings, boredom, or even abuse at the hands of the other. This check-off can help people distinguish between a temporary fascination and the presence of a lasting potential for mutual stimulation and growth.

Feeling consistently stimulated by the other person is also an important "equalizing" factor for relationships in which there's some kind of dramatic difference between the partners—for instance, an age gap of twenty years or more. A younger person of either gender may be intellectually stimulated by an older partner, but not have much to offer on that score in return. If the older person is drawn chiefly to the younger one's vitality, this may not prove to be a lasting trade-off. In any kind of relationship, there needs to be a roughly equal *learning exchange* going on between the partners, and the mutual feeling that both people will always be able to stimulate, provoke, and inform each other.

✔ *Is there something about the other person that makes you want to touch him or her tenderly?* This check-off is concerned with more than physical attraction alone. You might call it the "lust with trust" factor. Do you want to touch the other person respectfully? Do you think you will feel safe when he or she touches you? Do you feel a caring impulse along with some sexual desire?

While we've seen lots of people get involved sexually without much impulse toward caring, the reverse also happens sometimes—particularly with women who are uneasy about sex but used to performing in the role of caretaker. Thus it's not unusual to find unstable relationships in which the man is primarily involved for sex, and the woman is taking care of the emotional side of things. But a stable relationship needs sexual intimacy and caring to be intermingled for both partners. If you strongly feel one impulse but none of the other in a new relationship, be careful. It's not sufficient reason to call things off, but it is a sign that you should "go slow" with the development of intimacy until you feel a balance of lust and trust within yourself, and see reliable signs that the other person feels both as well.

When you're trying to determine whether to continue with a relationship at any stage, these four check-offs are essentials—like air, food, water, and shelter are essentials to life itself. If one or more of them are consistently out of kilter in a relationship, then you should do some serious thinking about why you are still pursuing the relationship, and what can be done to improve the inadequate factor(s). It's surprising how tenaciously people can sometimes hold onto relationships that are obviously deficient in some of these check-offs. More often than not that's a sign of their stubbornness and fuzzy vision, not their faith and determination. Faith and determination are what help you overlook and surpass less important imperfections in a relationship. Determining the right proportion of tolerable imperfections is the purpose of our next relationship-assessment factor.

THE WINGO 51-80 PRINCIPLE

We once asked 100 clients who had found successful relationships to list for us all the things they liked about their mates, and the things they would change about their mates if they could. When we compared everyone's responses, we found that there was an average of four items on the first list for each item on the second. This led us to conclude that successful relationships are based on a mutual "approval rating" of approximately 80 percent. That's the second part of our 51-80 Principle.

The first part is derived from our study of countless pieces of feedback, both on paper and in conversation, that our clients have given us about their first dates and the early stages of relationship. This feedback has led us to conclude that you need to find a little more than half—at least 51 percent—of the attributes you're looking for in a mate to keep a relationship going. Over time—roughly three to eighteen months—you want to see that percentage of desired attributes rising as you get to know a prospective mate better. When you can review your list and find that your partner seems strong on 80 percent of those desired attributes, it's probably time to bring up the subject of long-term commitment.

We introduce clients to the 51-80 Principle to counter two frequent errors that people make in assessing prospective life partners. The first error is looking for too much in the earliest stages of a relationship; the second error is expecting total perfection to develop in a later stage. When we introduce people to the 51 percent concept, they often protest to us, "But I want to get a lot more than half of the things I desire from a mate!" Anyone would, of course. But our point is that 51 percent may be fine in the earliest stages of getting to know each other. (If you think someone is 100 percent perfect after a first date, it's very unlikely that you've gotten the whole picture yet.) You can continue seeing that person in the hope that the 51 percent grows; as you near the time for commitment, 80 percent is the most you should require.

APPLYING THE 51-80 PRINCIPLE

To use this assessment method, you first have to know what you're looking for in a mate. That means thinking about it a little harder than most people do—hard enough to write up a list of all the attributes you would like to have in a mate. This is something you can do at any stage of a relationship search, and that you can continually revise in light of your experiences. When writing up a list, it's easiest at first just to write down one thing after another that comes to mind, until you feel that you've left no stone unturned. Then you can categorize what's on the list in a couple of different ways that we'll explain shortly.

First, let's look at a simulated list as an example. Imagine that Sylvia is a thirty-year-old legal assistant studying at night for the bar. Her life is understandably busy, even frantic at times, but she's recently made some time in her schedule to start looking for a mate. She's been divorced for three years and has a six-year-old son whom she cares for alone, as her ex-husband, Don, is across the continent. Reestablishing a stable family unit is very important to Sylvia, and thus so is a mate's maturity and steadfastness. Let's look over Sylvia's shoulder at the attributes that come to her mind as she imagines what an ideal mate would be like:

- Age: 35+
- Professional with an established career (but no lawyers!)
- Must like kids (and consider having one more with me)
- Healthy (no heart conditions, overweight, or anything like that)
- Nonsmoker
- Must have integrity, be truthful
- Must be friendly and sociable (no loners like Don)
- Romantic, fun-loving
- Makes at least $100,000 (I wish!)

- Able to talk about spiritual things, but not a religious fanatic
- Likes skiing *and* the beach
- Gentle, tolerant, doesn't judge people harshly
- Good-looking (but not attractive enough to get too much attention!)
- Likes to travel, do things, not just work all the time
- Optimistic, not down in the mouth
- Willing to share household duties (esp. cooking!)
- Supportive of my career, not afraid of it
- Politically aware and moderate (no political lectures!)
- Very sensual (yes! yes!)
- Athletic but not a sports junkie—likes to play family games, not just "hard" sports with other guys
- Reliable—will do what he says he will instead of just making promises
- Willing to talk things out, not hide his feelings
- Good sense of humor, but not a full-time joker (I hate that!)
- No big drinking habit (and no beer cans left around the house)
- Respectful of my women friends (and *must* like Sandra!)
- Must like animals and house pets, esp. cats
- Good taste in clothes, able to choose things for me (dream on)
- Likes baroque and chamber music
- Likes to take me out to dinner!

With twenty-nine preferences on her list, Sylvia has a strong, solid list to use in her later assessments of the men she meets. First, though, she needs to separate from this list the attributes that she believes she will be able to discern over the first three or four dates with a good prospect, and the attributes that will take longer to certify. This gives her a "short-term" and a "long-term" list:

Short Term

- Age 35+
- Professional with an established career (but no lawyers!)
- Must like kids (and consider having one more with me)
- Healthy (no heart conditions, overweight, or anything like that)
- Nonsmoker
- Must be friendly and sociable (no loners like Don)
- Likes baroque and chamber music
- Must like animals and house pets, esp. cats
- Likes to take me out to dinner!
- Romantic, fun-loving
- Makes at least $100,000 (I wish!)
- Able to talk about spiritual things, but not a religious fanatic
- Likes skiing *and* the beach
- Good-looking (but not attractive enough to get too much attention!)
- Likes to travel, do things, not just work all the time
- Politically aware and moderate (no political lectures!)
- Athletic but not a sports junkie—likes to play family games, not just "hard" sports with other guys

Long Term

- Good sense of humor, but not a full-time joker (I hate that!)
- No big drinking habit (and no beer cans left around the house)
- Must have integrity, be truthful
- Gentle, tolerant, doesn't judge people harshly
- Optimistic, not down in the mouth
- Willing to share household duties (esp. cooking!)
- Supportive of my career, not afraid of it
- Very sensual (yes! yes!)
- Reliable—will do what he says he will instead of just making promises
- Willing to talk things out, not hide his feelings
- Respectful of my women friends (and *must* like Sandra!)
- Good taste in clothes, able to choose things for me (dream on)

Notice that Sylvia's short-term list carries mostly factual characteristics and likes or dislikes that she can certify by asking questions and by her own observation. The long-term list carries attributes that can't be so quickly identified. For instance, Sylvia has put "very sensual" in her long-term list because she doesn't intend to have sexual relations with anyone over the short term. She also realizes that reliability, integrity, gentleness, and optimism are deep qualities of character that take time for her to be sure of. And, of course, she can't know if a man is willing to do his share of household chores until she's living with him.

At this point, Sylvia decides to further refine both lists by making notations to herself about which attributes she considers essential to a successful relationship, and which would be nice to have but are optional. She denotes her choices by marking them E (essential) or O (optional). Now let's take a look at both lists again for a picture of Sylvia's real priorities:

Short Term

E • Age 35+

E • Professional with an established career (but no lawyers!)

E • Must like kids (and consider having one more with me)

E • Healthy (no heart conditions, overweight, or anything like that)

E • Nonsmoker

E • Must be friendly and sociable (no loners like Don)

O • Likes baroque and chamber music

O • Must like animals and house pets, esp. cats

O • Likes to take me out to dinner!

E • Romantic, fun-loving

O • Makes at least $100,000 (I wish!)

O • Able to talk about spiritual things, but not a religious fanatic

O • Likes skiing *and* the beach

E • Good-looking (but not attractive enough to get too much attention!)

E • Likes to travel, do things, not just work all the time

O • Politically aware and moderate (no political lectures!)

O • Athletic but not a sports junkie—likes to play family games, not just "hard" sports with other guys

Long Term

E • Good sense of humor, but not a full-time joker
(I hate that!)

E • No big drinking habit (and no beer cans left around
the house)

E • Must have integrity, be truthful

E • Gentle, tolerant, doesn't judge people harshly

E • Optimistic, not down in the mouth

E • Willing to share household duties (esp. cooking!)

E • Supportive of my career, not afraid of it

E • Very sensual (yes! yes!)

E • Reliable—will do what he says he will instead of just
making promises

E • Willing to talk things out, not hide his feelings

E • Respectful of my women friends (and *must* like
Sandra!)

O • Good taste in clothes, able to choose things for me
(dream on)

A few weeks after sorting out these two lists, Sylvia meets Bruce, a thirty-seven-year-old art director for a city magazine. She goes out with him four times over the next couple of months, and feels increasingly fond of him. But she wants to balance her feelings with a more rational analysis, and so she turns to her short-term list of desired attributes to see whether Bruce is really measuring up. Let's look at what she checks off:

Short Term

✓ • Age 35+

✓ • Professional with an established career (but no
lawyers!)

- Must like kids (and consider having one more with me)
✓ • Healthy (no heart conditions, overweight, or anything like that)
✓ • Nonsmoker
✓ • Must be friendly and sociable (no loners like Don)
- Likes baroque and chamber music
- Must like animals and house pets, esp. cats
✓ • Likes to take me out to dinner!
✓ • Romantic, fun-loving
- Makes at least $100,000 (I wish!)
✓ • Able to talk about spiritual things, but not a religious fanatic
1/2 ✓ • Likes skiing *and* the beach
✓ • Good-looking (but not attractive enough to get too much attention!)
✓ • Likes to travel, do things, not just work all the time
- Politically aware and moderate (no political lectures!)
- Athletic but not a sports junkie—likes to play family games, not just "hard" sports with other guys
✓ • Very good taste in art—a great decorator!

Notice that Sylvia is stacking the deck a little bit in Bruce's favor by adding a quality she likes about him but hadn't been looking for in a mate. This is okay, as long as one doesn't deliberately add a lot of qualities to counterbalance a high proportion of negatives. At any rate, Sylvia finds that Bruce has 11 1/2 of 18 qualities on her short-term "want list," for a percentage of 64. In balance with her feelings for Bruce, this gives her a clear go-ahead message about the relationship.

But she will need to reflect on the attributes she marked earlier as "essential" that Bruce is not yet showing. For instance, he's made it clear that he's ambivalent about having any children of his own, and while he's been friendly to Sylvia's little boy in two meetings, it's hard for her to tell whether the two of them will really hit it off. Possibly Sylvia will realize that she's misplaced this item, and that it really belongs on the long-term list. It may be too much to ask of a man that he show certainty on this issue during the earliest phase of a relationship. Realizing this may reveal some of Sylvia's impatience and anxiety about this issue to herself.

This kind of factor demonstrates a hidden purpose of the 51-80 Principle—it helps you get to know yourself better at the same time that it helps you assess the desirable qualities of a prospective mate. That's why you should keep your list and categories open to revision, amendments, and deletions. And remember at all times that this kind of assessment is only a rational tool that's to be used in balance with your feelings and intuition about a developing relationship. While we occasionally meet someone who is *too* rational in their approach to intimacy, we find that most people go with their feelings and intuition but very little rational assessment. Some of those people suffer for lacking the latter point of view.

Let's assume that after six more months, Sylvia and Bruce had been sexually intimate for a while and spend so much time together that they are discussing the possibility of setting up house. Sylvia returns to her lists, rearranges them a little, and comes up with the following assessment:

Short Term

✓ • Age 35+
✓ • Professional with an established career (but no lawyers!)
✓ • Healthy (no heart conditions, overweight, or anything like that)
✓ • Nonsmoker
✓ • Must be friendly and sociable (no loners like Don)
    • Likes baroque and chamber music
1/2✓ • Must like animals and house pets, esp. cats
✓ • Likes to take me out to dinner!
✓ • Romantic, fun-loving
    • Makes at least $100,000 (I wish!)
✓ • Able to talk about spiritual things, but not a religious fanatic
1/2✓ • Likes skiing *and* the beach
✓ • Good-looking (but not attractive enough to get too much attention!)
✓ • Likes to travel, do things, not just work all the time
1/2✓ • Politically aware and moderate (no political lectures!)
1/2✓ • Athletic but not a sports junkie—likes to play family games, not just "hard" sports with other guys
✓ • Very good taste in art—a great decorator!

Long Term

1/2✓ • Must like kids (and consider having one more with me)
1/2✓ • Good sense of humor, but not a full-time joker (I hate that!)
✓ • No big drinking habit (and no beer cans left around the house)

✓ • Must have integrity, be truthful
✓ • Gentle, tolerant, doesn't judge people harshly
✓ • Optimistic, not down in the mouth
✓ • Willing to share household duties (esp. cooking!)
✓ • Supportive of my career, not afraid of it
✓ • Very sensual (yes! yes!)
✓ • Reliable—will do what he says he will instead of just making promises
✓ • Willing to talk things out, not hide his feelings
✓ • Respectful of my women friends (and *must* like Sandra!)
!✓ • Good taste in clothes, able to choose things for me (dream on)

Based on her better knowledge of Bruce, Sylvia now gives him a total of 25 points out of a possible 30—a score of 83 percent. Note that she finds him strong on most of the long-term essentials. But he's still not a natural with her son, and she gives him only a half point on his sense of humor because he tends to be a little solemn. On the first list, he's turned out to be neither particularly athletic nor politically concerned, but Sylvia was unsure of just how much these factors counted with her anyway. All in all, if we reviewed such an assessment with a client like Sylvia, we'd advise her to proceed with discussions and plans for a long-term commitment, as long as she felt a growing affection and respect for her partner. All the signs point toward a lasting love.

SEXUAL TIMING

A plainspoken woman who had just signed on to our program once said to John, "For what I'm paying you I want some hard answers to specific questions. How long should a woman wait before sleeping with a guy she's met?"

"Well," John replied, "that depends on a lot of factors, especially the quality of communication between the people involved. But if you're asking for general advice, we'd say that a good rule of thumb is to wait until you've had six dates over a couple of months."

"Really?!" the woman replied, obviously shocked. "That's not what I've always believed."

"And what's that?" John inquired.

"Well, it's always been my firm policy *never* to sleep with a man until the second date."

"Where did you learn that policy?"

"I guess it's what I learned at college from my sorority sisters. The rule was, sex on the first date meant you were loose, but by the second date the guy needs to know whether you're really interested—right?"

John smiled wryly and replied, "Well, I bet the frat boys loved to visit your sorority house, didn't they?"

The woman grinned and admitted, "Yes, they did, as a matter of fact."

When, where, and how to initiate sexual relations is a very sensitive subject for which there really are no hard answers. The factors of age, emotional readiness, physical condition, religious beliefs, and mutual sensuality are just too variable from couple to couple to allow for a fail-safe formula or guideline. Nonetheless, people often ask us what we think is safe and sensible, and that's why we give them our rule-of-thumb answer. We'll explain the reasoning behind it shortly. But first let's look at four scenarios, all based on real encounters, that show how differing timetables for sexual intimacy work (or don't work) in different circumstances.

Beginners Luck

Bob, thirty-four, and Janelle, thirty, are set up by mutual friends for a blind-date lunch on a Saturday. Both divorced and alone for the last several years, they are eager for a relationship but understandably nervous about this kind of meeting. However, things go exceedingly well. The two find a lot to talk and laugh about, and they're still wrapped up in conversation when the cafe closes down at four p.m. So Bob invites Janelle for a walk down by the waterfront. Once Janelle trips on a sidewalk broken by a tree root, Bob catches her, and presto—they're holding hands for the rest of their walk. Near sundown, Bob boldly but gently embraces Janelle and gives her a kiss on the cheek. When she only blushes in response, Bob says, "Let's go to dinner, okay?" They do that, and catch a movie, then wind up in a quiet hotel bar, giggling and snuggling together in a dark corner for an hour and a half. Finally Janelle whispers, "This is ridiculous. Can we go to your place?"

The next day Janelle's friend calls her and asks, "Well, how did it go? Do you think I might have made a good match for you?"

Janelle, embarrassed, replies, "Oh, maybe. He seems nice. I'll let you know." Bob and Janelle begin dating steadily, but they don't let their friends in on just how quickly their match "took" until their engagement party one year later.

Taking a Chance

Loren, twenty-six, is a roving geologist for an oil company. Since college she's traveled the world but had no intimate relationships, and hasn't yet married when she meets Arnie, thirty-six, an ex-Marine and successful entrepreneur. They have a delightful time on their first date, until the very end when Arnie says, "Look, Loren, I have to make a trip to Denver two weekends from now for a Friday night meeting. I can't get a decent flight back until Monday, and it seems like such a waste to fly two thousand miles for one meeting. Would you like to come along for a ski weekend? I know this is rather sudden, but I have to make my plans now. I'd really like to see you again before we go, and you can cancel at any time, no questions asked. How about it?"

Feeling very warm toward Arnie but slightly terrified by the implications of his invitation, Loren is speechless at first. Finally she smiles and says, "No questions asked, really?"

"Really," Arnie assures her. They do meet twice more before their trip together, and they make love in the hotel on their first night in Denver. Three months later, they're happily living together.

Taking It Slow

Darren, fifty-nine, is a former major league baseball player and owner of a very successful and reputable automobile dealership. At a picnic given by his sister he meets

Hope, a fifty-one-year-old widow with two grown children who administers a charitable organization owned by her church, a Unitarian denomination. Describing herself as a "religious freethinker," Hope fascinates Darren with the stories of her wild youth, and she's slightly embarrassed to realize how attracted she is to Darren's still-athletic poise and strength. Both of them have recently been through painful dissolutions of marriages: Darren's first and only, dating back to his twenties, and Hope's second, of fifteen years duration. Each of them has reason to be emotionally tentative in their first few dates. So they see each other mostly in the company of other friends, and Darren starts helping out in Hope's charity on the weekends. Six weeks go by before they even kiss—and four months pass, encompassing twenty or so "dates," before they drive off to spend a romantic weekend together. Darren proposes marriage to Hope that weekend, and they both agree that sex is a very precious thing that they can both wait a little longer for. They do—until the next night.

A Wound Unhealed

Lana, twenty-seven, is a tall and athletic L.A. blonde—in fact, she's the captain of a world-class women's volleyball team that frequently travels abroad for competitions. In the process of pursuing corporate sponsorship for her team, she meets Eric, thirty, an advertising man in Toronto who's on the mend from a broken heart. Three months ago he discovered that his long-time girlfriend had never been true to him, having had two or three secret affairs over the last six years. Emotionally devastated, Eric began having problems with sexual intimacy in the waning stages of his relationship, which the girlfriend wanted to continue after her confessions. But he finally broke it off during a wrenching fight, and has sworn off romances for a while. But, feeling lonely and vulnerable, Eric is powerfully drawn to Lana's sunny nature and strong, athletic physicality. Both outdoors people, they spend their first three dates swimming, cycling, and running together—although these dates take place weeks apart, considering the distance to be covered between Canada and California.

Eight weeks after they met, Lana calls Eric long-distance and asks him if he'd like to meet her in Seattle where she has a game the next week. "I'd love to have a wrestling match with you in the Hilton's honeymoon suite," she laughs, making her intentions quite clear. But Eric mumbles, "Maybe this is a little premature," and Lana backs off. Two meetings and another month later, she's a little more forceful.

"Look, Eric, I don't mind saying I want to sleep with you. It's important to me that we develop this part of our relationship. Am I not attractive enough for you?"

"Oh, no," Eric replies helplessly. "You're just great. It's really me who's the problem—I don't know if I could do anything even if we got into bed."

"Well, why don't we give it a chance," Lana says gently.

"No," Eric says. "Please, I just don't feel right about it." Lana leaves disappointed, and Eric realizes morosely that he's still hurting too much about his recent past to be getting involved sexually with anyone. Though the two of them talk twice more by phone, the energy seems to have gone out of their relationship. Lana cancels their next scheduled meeting, and they drift apart.

DEVELOPING SEXUAL DISCRETION

What did you feel and think as you read through the preceding scenarios? Were you worried, shocked, favorably impressed, or angry with the behavior of any of the characters? What might you have done differently if you were in any of their shoes?

One positive reason that almost everyone is fascinated with the gossip about others' sexual lives is that it gives us a chance to imagine ourselves in similar situations, and to imagine how we might respond to circumstances we've never faced in our own lives. Talking about sexual choices and ways of being can be a valuable part of developing sexual discretion, if we approach such talk in an open-minded and unafraid manner. Our culture is much more open about sex than it used to be, and the silver lining to the dark cloud of AIDS is that our openness and cultural awareness about many sexual issues is being accelerated by the necessity of a greater common knowledge.

Our first piece of advice about the timing of sexual intimacy in a developing relationship is to make sure you've given the subject enough thought to *have* some personal discretion—instead of just following rules you learned in college, or from your parents, church, or peers. While you might eventually decide on your own that the moral or religious directives you were taught are worth following, it's important to be able to explain to yourself, or a prospective sexual partner, *why* they are worth following. Otherwise your unexamined beliefs may crumble under the pressure of someone's unscrupulous seduction, and you will find yourself with no moral compass whatsoever.

By and large, however, we see a greater number of

clients (particularly men, it must be said) whose sexual discretion can be summarized by the motto, "As soon as possible under any circumstances." The spectre of AIDS has definitely tempered this attitude, but it's still very evident out there in the singles scene. The problem with this attitude is not just that it encourages premature sexual intimacy, but also that it tends to be selfishly oriented, inconsiderate of other people's needs, and ignorant of all the more subtle energies that need to develop slowly in a relationship to support a loving sexual intimacy. The "sex ASAP" attitude can thus substantially disrupt or even fatally wound the slowly developing care and tenderness of an intimate partnership, creating regrets or resentments that can become chronic problems between two people later on. While whirlwind scenarios such as Bob's and Janelle's do happen, to no one's detriment, they require rare alignments of two people's emotional needs and sexual readiness. Certainly such encounters are not to be planned or expected.

Our rule of thumb about "six dates over a couple of months" before sexual intimacy balances a practical realism about the sexual impatience of modern human beings with a measure of restraint—restraint that's a little greater than we see in most of our clients, particularly those under age forty-five. Again, it's not a hard-and-fast rule that you should accept without questioning. Rather, it's a suggestion that's worth comparing to your own experience and your sense of what's right. As a guideline for the perplexed, pressured or unprepared, we have no reservation in recommending it.

SEXUAL ETIQUETTE

There's enough information readily available on the issues of sexual etiquette to make detailed suggestions redundant. A few general principles to remember are:

1. Talk about AIDS and other sexually related diseases before intimacy. Two people who respect each other should have no trouble agreeing to tests that will provide reasonable assurance that they both have clean bills of health. If someone flatly refuses a test without a good explanation, regard him or her as a high risk and act accordingly. If you're getting ready to have sex but don't feel ready to talk about these subjects, then you're jumping the gun in an assuredly dangerous way. Besides the safety issue, you could be setting a precedent for developing other kinds of intimacy, from emotional to financial, without thorough mutual discussion of the issues involved.

2. Contraception and sexual safety is not a "woman's responsibility" or a "man's responsibility." It is the responsibility of anyone who intends to have sex. Don't expect a prospective partner to take care of it for you. However, early on in your sexual relationship you should discuss ways of sharing the responsibility with your partner.

3. Sex should never be used as leverage, for example, "I need you to sleep with me to prove this relationship means something to you." If you are tempted to express this attitude, question your motives. If you are confronted with such a challenge, politely refuse to cooperate. Remember that sexual intimacy is part of a naturally developing, mutually respectful relationship—not "proof" of love. The difference is a matter of patience; as we've said earlier in this book, "Patience = Respect."

4. *In all circumstances, sexual refusal by either person should be respectfully accepted.* Even if you think you are being teased, it's smarter not to play the game than to become aggressive. If someone is often using sexual refusal as reverse leverage, that is, to gain power over you, this calls for counseling together, not brute force.

5. *It's better to discuss preferences* about sexual practices, positions, and sensations than simply to assume that your partner will know everything that you like. If you are embarrassed about bringing up such issues, there are more than enough explicit sex manuals that you can use to spark the discussion.

WARNING SIGNS OF UNHEALTHY RELATING

In the next chapter we're going to discuss the most important issues of making the transition from a developing relationship to a committed one. Before we do, however, we feel it's necessary to discuss briefly some of the warning signs of unhealthy relating—signals that may help you avert a painful breakup after a commitment has been made, or simply help you keep your relationship evolving in a healthy direction. As a rule, these are things to keep in mind after you've been seeing someone steadily for at least a couple of months, after the first bloom of romance has subsided and your relationship has taken on a certain pattern and sense of reliability. Five signs to watch out for:

Chronic selfishness of either partner. Is the other person giving off consistent evidence that their interests are more important than yours? Do you ever feel "left out" of mutual plans and decision making? Do you always end up talking more about the other person's problems and concerns than yours? Be sure to put the shoe on the other foot, too, and ask yourself if your partner ever complains about being ignored or seems to be nagging for your attention all the time. There's probably a reason.

Codependency. If you're not sure what this is, a quick trip to the bookstore will fill in the blanks for you. There are more self-help books available on this issue than there are sex manuals these days! In shorthand, however, the signals of codependency are: expecting someone to "save your life" (or believing that your partner couldn't possibly survive without you); making excuses for your partner's self-destructive behavior (or expecting your partner to excuse yours); and generally *leaning* on each other more than you are *learning* from each other. Healthy dependence means expecting each other to help both of you toward greater self-acceptance, deeper maturity, and expanded capabilities. Codependency means helping each other stay immature, trapped in self-defeating habits or beliefs, and pessimistic about the future.

Declining mutual interest. If your lust remains high but you and your partner have less and less to talk about as the months go by, this is a sign that you need to reconsider the foundations of your relationship. Some couples settle for a chiefly sexual bond or become adjusted to living separate lives in close proximity, because they neither want to confront their problems nor want to suffer the disruption of going their separate ways. These situations are not hard to recognize; they're just difficult to admit and change. Who doesn't know someone with a "trophy wife" or a husband of convenience? And who doesn't know such a partnership to be chronically unhappy?

Isolated lifestyle as a couple. By contrast, some people can form such an intense partnership that they increasingly exclude prior friends and relatives from their social circle—until that circle is nothing more than a tight rubber band making them inseparable from each other. Occasionally we see two people who were each suspicious of humanity in general before they met, and who decide while falling in love that an "us against the world" stance is their best bet for making their future work. This is really a way of defending each other's low self-esteem by placing the specialness of their partnership above the welfare of everyone else—a special form of codependency. In the long run, however, this kind of passionate isolation will prove brittle, and its disintegration can be devastating to the individuals involved.

Chronic compatibility struggles. Are you trying to make two clashing lifestyles merge when they're not likely to? Perhaps a party animal and a monk bump into each other on the street and, fascinated by the differences between them, fall into a passionate embrace and thereafter expect love to work out all their contradictions. Well, it just may not work out that way. Signs of a chronic struggle for compatibility include having to make up excuses for the relationship to concerned friends or relatives, and/or an expectation that things will miraculously improve on their own: "We won't have these problems once we get married." Don't count on it.

How can you prevent these warning signs of unhealthy relating? We advise checking frequently on the quality of your relationship with our four check-offs and the 51-80 Principle. How can you work on these problems once they've already become apparent? For the most part, the answer to that is the pursuit of better communication skills that will help you keep two-way intimacy vital and ripening. We'll give you some goals for communication in our next and final chapter.

7

Deciding for Devotion: How to Approach the Issues of Commitment

*I chose my wife, as she did her wedding gown,
not for a fine glossy surface, but such qualities
as would wear well.*

—Oliver Goldsmith

*"Now what do I do?" said the panicked voice on the line to
Julie. "This month I've had dates with both of the men you
picked for me—and they've both proposed!"*

*The voice belonged to May, a very attractive forty-four-
year-old Japanese-American woman who had come to us
about six weeks earlier. Tiny, demure, and always fastidi-
ously dressed, May had been a bundle of nerves in her interview. She had kept apologizing just for being there: "I'm
sorry, I don't know what else to do. My husband died two
years ago after we'd been together for twenty years, and I
never dated anyone else. I was in America only three years before I met Chad; I was just a little girl really. Looking for a
husband is all so new to me, I don't know if I will be able to
help you very much. I'm sorry."*

We had assured May that we were there to help her, not

187

the other way around, and that she had a lot going for her in the search for a new mate. She looked six or seven years younger than her age, with delicate features and a graceful poise that seemed more Oriental than American. Yet she had been Westernized enough to develop a degree of independence that wasn't immediately discernible in her looks and her social style. May had experienced a happy and devoted marriage that produced one son, now in college, and she was financially self-sufficient from her half-time career as a medical researcher and some good investment properties. She had no ambivalence about wanting to find a new life partner, and she had an experienced understanding of the marriage commitment.

After our initial talk with May, the two of us discussed a mutual concern that we had not brought up with May since she had seemed consumed with worry already. The problem was that May was so attractive, and at least initially deferential to men, that she might draw a lot more attention from male prospects than she was ready for. And not all that attention might be trustworthy.

We tried to counter this hazard by starting our candidate search with men fifty and above who had expressed no obsessive interest in a much younger mate. We wanted to match May with mature men who weren't in the throes of a mid-life crisis, and who could measure up to her in terms of reliability and responsibility. Then we did a further scan for men in this age range who were widowers, since it's usually a little easier for people who have experienced the same kind of loss to understand each other's feelings as they move toward a new intimacy.

The first candidate, Alan, seemed to fit all the criteria, although his wife had died ten years earlier and he'd had one serious, nonmarried relationship since. At fifty-three, he was an executive vice-president of a rock-solid international shipping firm, and he seemed to embody the conservative values that his position in the business world implied. He had told us that he liked to make big decisions cautiously, weighing all the relevant factors over as much time as possible, and that he intended to conduct the search for a marriage partner in the same way. We thought Alan's stability and conscious deliberation might be a good counterbalance to May's current uncertainty and anxiety.

The man whom May met second, Warren, was a forty-nine-year-old administrator of an arts institute, roughly equal in professional stature to Alan but from a very different world. His values were more liberal and his social world definitely more offbeat. His wife had died a few years earlier after a long struggle with cancer. Like Alan, Warren told us he wanted to take things slowly, at least in terms of meeting women, and thus May was only the second prospect he had met through our program within the first three months. Warren seemed trustworthy and honorable, but he was a little harder to pin down than Alan. He had a more mercurial nature, and there seemed to us a possibility that he might seem a little unmanageable in May's eyes. Her scientific bent and love of order suggested that she might be a little overcontrolling in a relationship, and Warren was used to a world of creativity and ongoing near-chaos.

May met Alan and Warren within two days of each other, and we thought that the clear differences between them would at least help her establish a sense of direction for her partner search. But by the time she called us with precocious proposals from both men on the table, she seemed totally unable to distinguish any preference within herself. As we'd suspected, May's attractiveness had clearly overwhelmed the "go slow" attitude of both men, and so we advised her not to accept either proposal anytime soon. In fact, Julie advised May over the phone that there was no reason she couldn't continue to see both men for a while, politely postponing consideration of their proposals for the time being.

The suggestion shocked May. "Oh no, I couldn't do that!" she exclaimed. "I think I should develop things with only one of them, so that neither one feels that I'm leading him on."

"All right," agreed Julie, "you should follow what you think is right. So which fellow do you think it will be?"

"I don't have the slightest idea," May confessed. "They both seem like very nice men."

Further discussion revealed that May's appraisal of each man didn't go much deeper than "very nice," and so Julie reminded her of our four check-offs and the 51-80 Principle as means she could use to specify her desires and compare the two men. She promised she would, but we had our doubts about how thorough she had been when she called Julie back a few days later.

"Well, I've made my choice of who to continue going out with," May proudly told Julie.

"Who's the lucky guy?"

"I think it will have to be Alan."

"And what made you pick him?"

"It's only fair," May said decisively. *"He called me first."*

No doubt it was May's difficulty in deciding what was important to her personally that made her unusually dependent on our advice for the next few months. Always concerned primarily with what was right or proper to do, she called us about every other day, it seemed, to ask our opinion about something that was happening in her relationship with Alan. Should she buy a formal gown for the New Year's ball at Alan's firm? Should she go along on a weekend trip with him and his grown children after only four dates? How should she reply to Warren's periodic inquiries about how she was doing? Every time we tried to help May assess her own feelings about these issues, she seemed dissatisfied. Whenever she felt uncertain, she simply wanted someone to tell her what to do. Sometimes we gave her a definite suggestion; sometimes we didn't.

Finally, May snagged John on the phone one day after she'd been dating Alan for about three months. She sounded unusually down and doubtful. *"John, I asked Alan last night if his proposal was still in effect. I thought that maybe I've been seeing him long enough to talk about the future. Was that right?"*

"That depends in part on what Alan said," John suggested.

"That's what's confusing to me," May replied. *"It seemed that when I met Alan, he wanted to marry me the next week. But last night we said he didn't think we should be rushing into anything. He said he'd like to give our rela-*

tionship at least two years before we decide. That seems like a long time, doesn't it?"

"Well, frankly I don't like the sound of it," John remarked. "May, you don't have to answer this if you don't want to, but it would help to know whether you've become intimate with Alan yet."

There was a pause on the other end of the line, and then an embarrassed sigh. "No, but he's pushing for it," May said in a near-whisper. "That's one of the reasons I brought up the proposal again, I guess."

"I see," John said as neutrally as possible, although he was feeling increasingly troubled by what he was hearing. Although he remembered Alan's preference for taking things slowly, it seemed that Alan was changing his story with May to suit his desires at the time. "How do you feel about becoming intimate with Alan before marriage?" John asked. "Would it feel like the right thing to do?"

"Oh, I don't know," she answered tentatively. "I guess I feel a little pressured. He said he needed to know that we were going somewhere, and I don't want him to think I'm cold. But last night I wondered if something about having sex would make him want to put everything on hold for a while. He was a little mysterious."

That was all John needed to hear to solidify his doubts about this relationship. It wasn't the first time he had heard of men offering marriage proposals to speed up the process of sexual intimacy, only to back away and slow things down once sex had been initiated. It seemed distinctly possible to John that Alan was entertaining the idea of starting a sexual relationship with May without committing to marriage.

He was probably more interested in control than commitment, and that meant he wasn't really ready for a new permanent relationship.

Thus, it seemed important to John that May take some measures to protect herself. He suggested that she think carefully about whether she would feel comfortable in a sexual relationship with Alan. If she didn't, John advised her, she should tell Alan that she wanted to cool things off while they both thought more about their marriage potential.

"Can I do that?" May asked in a surprised tone.

"Of course you can," John affirmed. "You can and should do anything that makes you feel more comfortable in the relationship. And pay close attention to how Alan takes it. If he really respects you, he'll be considerate of your needs. If he gets angry or tries to pressure you in any way, you may want to give this whole relationship another look. In my opinion, you should think about seeing other men on a casual basis. We can always line up a new prospect for you."

"Well, Warren keeps calling me back every two weeks," May revealed. "I'm beginning to feel bad because I keep making excuses not to meet him for lunch."

"Why don't you give him a call then?" suggested John. "I think he's a trustworthy guy, and it seems obvious that he's still interested in you even though you chose Alan over him. Now you can make a little better comparison of the two. Just make a casual lunch date. It doesn't have to be anything heavy."

"But what do I tell Alan?" May asked worriedly.

"You don't have to tell him anything about seeing another guy at lunch," replied John. "If it really bothers you or

193

it turns out you'd like to see more of Warren, just tell Alan that you're not going to close down all your options for the next two years without a good reason. One way or another, I think that it will make Alan's real intentions clear."

Three weeks later, May called John back and said, "How did you know what would happen? I've seen Warren twice and had a wonderful time on both dates. When I told Alan I felt uncomfortable about our having sex without a firmer commitment, he became very surly and stood me up for our next date. So I'm just not going to bother with him. He always seemed a little stodgy, if you know what I mean."

Four months later, we stood up for Warren and May at their private wedding ceremony, and joined them and their children for a sailboat celebration on San Francisco Bay. May later revealed to us that Warren had agreed that the two of them should hold off on sex until they were married, and this had made her feel much safer and more secure as their relationship developed. Theirs was not the optimal pairing we might have predicted at the beginning of May's program, and May had to experience the contrast between two available men over time to distinguish her real needs and preferences. When she saw the difference in respect she received from these two, she knew which one offered the qualities that would wear well in a lasting relationship.

TAKING THE BIG STEP

When people are making the transition from dating steadily to creating a committed relationship, they are prone to one of two common errors: 1) not waiting long enough to be certain their relationship has what it will take to last, and 2) waiting too long. Some people make the first mistake because they are so insecure alone that they will rush to firm up a new relationship that shows any potential whatsoever, even if that potential equals nothing more than a casual friendship. Although it is not so common anymore, we have also seen people rush into marriage because their moral or religious upbringing has convinced them they should not have sex beforehand, yet their lust eventually overcomes their better judgment about the relationship as a whole. Finally, there are people who are so used to "revolving door" marriages that it's not a serious matter for them to tie the knot in Vegas on one besotted weekend and untie it a couple of years or even a few months later.

Waiting too long to commit is a cultural trend that has largely developed over the last four or five decades, along with the changing social roles of men and women and our evolving ideas about what a marriage or committed relationship is for. Those of us raised on the notion of romantic devotion don't always appreciate its novelty in human history. It was not so long ago that most marriages were either formally arranged or dictated by the needs of a couple's families and the immediate social environment in which they grew up. As our society became less community-bound and individuals began to live their lives mostly independent of their roots, people started marrying chiefly for personal and subjective reasons—or as some might put it, "only for love."

Marrying for love seems right and natural to most of us nowadays. But it's complicated by another change in our culture—an obsession with sexual romance that has been raised to a fever pitch by our advertising, entertainment, and popular literature. Many young hearts are broken as people learn that sexual romance and love are not entirely synonymous; although the first can lead to the second, it's not inevitable. A tragic number of people become so addicted to the exciting high of sexual romance that they never get around to making the *decision* to love someone beyond that stage.

Hence we see a lot of divorces that occur at the point when sexual romance has dimmed somewhat and a deliberate decision for love has not taken root. We also hear of many people who go from one sexually romantic affair to another, leaving whenever the initial excitement begins to wane and constantly searching for a "love high" that will last forever. This is the chief cause of people who are in workable relationships waiting too long to commit. You can bet that at least one of the partners is imagining that another romantic affair awaits them where the effortless ecstasy of falling in love will last much longer, and the hard work of a committed relationship will be much easier.

Part of our business consists of reminding people of what goes into the decision to build a lasting love. There are rational, material, and practical elements to be considered along with emotional, sexual, and mystical elements. We don't tell people very much about handling the mystical elements; they pretty much take care of themselves. But we give people our four check-offs and the 51-80 Principle to help them remember the more down-to-earth elements of relationship at every stage. And when people who have been dating seriously for a while begin to ask us about the rational and material issues of commitment, we talk to them about the following list.

THE MAJOR ISSUES OF COMMITMENT

Mutual Expectations

This commitment issue comes first because it affects all the rest. We've heard countless stories about failed marriages that begin with words like "Marriage was certainly not what I expected" or "I never expected a husband/wife of mine to [*do something unexpected*]!" We fear that a shocking number of couples never overtly discuss their private expectations about what will happen after marrying or moving in together, with the result that disappointment and disillusionment are sure to follow.

In general, we've observed that women are a little more prone to unreasonable or even magical expectations about what marriage will do for them: "If I get married I can quit this job I hate"; "I'll be able to lose weight once we're married"; "He won't sleep around after we're married," etc. Men's expectations are often more self-serving. They may confidently anticipate that a woman will provide a free maid service for them, even if she's shown no proclivity for housecleaning in her single life. Or men will blithely assume that their careers will take precedence over their mate's if any conflict arises.

People of both sexes are prone to expect marriage or commitment to automatically solve problems that destroyed former relationships. "I could never talk to my first wife," a client once complained to us, adding that he hoped we could find for him "a woman who's easier to talk to." When we asked if he had done anything to improve *his* personal communication skills since his divorce, he was offended.

197

Often it seems that people regard the marriage vows as some kind of magical incantation that will effect dramatic changes in their personalities, habits, and relationship patterns that they haven't been able to make by any other means. But marriage is not an easy route to wish fulfillment. It *is* a way for two people to dedicate themselves to working together to change and deepen their lives. But one should never assume that marriage alone will change anyone's basic character over the short term. Marriage will change both partners positively over the long term only if that's their serious mutual intent. And if one marries only for security and stasis—that is, in order *not* to change— then one's character is likely to deteriorate over time, as well as the quality of the partnership.

It's less important that all your expectations be sensible than that you share them openly with your intended partner before a firm relationship commitment is made. In healthy relationships, the expectations of each person will naturally surface in conversation over time, and can be respectfully acknowledged and negotiated, if necessary. If you find yourself withholding an expectation or you sense that your partner is not telling you something important that he or she desires from the future, don't let that situation go on for too long. It's far better to tackle such awkward topics before you've pledged your faith to each other than to marry and then wait suspensefully to see if you get what you want, or if your partner has a big surprise for you. The healthiest situation shortly before marriage is for two people to have expectations that truly are mutual, because they've been thoroughly discussed and harmonized as much as possible.

Present and Future Families

We've observed that younger people are more likely to discuss carefully and plan for their upcoming family than older people are to talk over the potential effects of a new partnership on the children they already have. "I hope my kids approve of my fiancée," a fifty-five-year-old executive with two children in their early twenties told us. "If not, the hell with them." We pointed out that he might not appreciate this attitude coming in his direction from his kids when they decided to get married, and he got the message. Like it or not, no pairing of two people, however passionate or seemingly perfect, comes without strings attached to relatives and close friends who will have a wide variety of opinions on the quality of the match. We advise our older clients with children from previous relationships to be sensitive to all the people their new relationship will affect, and to make some effort to mend fences as necessary before remarrying in order to preempt future frictions.

Our expertise does not lie in family planning or psychology, so we limit our advice to people anticipating children to match their expectations on the subject. Many loving couples nowadays are out of sync on this subject for a while, and we urge patience, caution, and good communication until both people are ready to move ahead. Having children should never be seen as a solution to chronic problems in relating, nor as a way to relieve pressure from relatives or peers to start a family. Now more than ever kids need loving, stable homes founded on the healthy partnership of their parents. There are more than enough people in the world, and far too many unwanted kids, for procreation

199

to be undertaken without an attitude of readiness, devotion, and hope for the future.

Finances

Most of our clients have more complicated financial situations than the prototypical young couple who marry in college and use old milk crates for furniture until they can build a solid financial foundation together. Many people nowadays are more close-mouthed about their financial profile than they are about their sexual lives, but secretiveness about money is a disastrous policy in an intimate relationship. This includes secretiveness in expectations, as when one person with significantly fewer resources expects his or her wealthier partner to pay off debts after marriage that haven't been mentioned beforehand.

The guideline for handling finances together is simple: Tell the whole truth about what you possess and expect to give or receive, and get professional or legal assistance to figure out what to do together about complications such as taxes, estates, insurance, investments, inheritances, bequests, and so forth. You may want to negotiate a prenuptial agreement about the sharing of resources, or at least come to a definite agreement about whether you will pool your checking and savings accounts, etc. There's no right way to manage all these affairs; there's only the way that both of you feel comfortable with after full and open discussion. You may also decide that one or the other of you is more competent to handle financial matters over the long term. If so, make sure you have regular check-ins with each other (every three to six months), and/or competent accounting or legal assistance, to protect the interests of the person who's not in charge of finances should the person taking care of it die unexpectedly.

Career and Role Compatibility

This issue is related to personal finances and is connected to the broader social questions of changing sex roles and professional equality as well. These days most couples can't make it without each partner working, and that fact brings up a whole host of potential problems to be negotiated. Some of the questions we've seen clients of all ages struggling with include:

Can we afford for me to stay at home and raise kids on my husband's salary?

If she makes more money than I do, is she in charge around the house?

If only one of us is a wage earner, how do we share the income?

Whose career should be sacrificed if one of us is transferred for a promotion?

Should we live in a place better for his career or mine?

If I'm ready to retire and travel and she's just starting a second career, how will we work out our time together?

How should we compensate for the fact that I have a rewarding career with a future and my partner has to work at a dead-end job to help us make ends meet?

If I pay for his schooling, should I ask for a guarantee that he'll pay me back if we ever divorce?

Can we really afford for her to quit work and try to write a novel?

Our answer to these and a host of other potential questions about careers and roles: Work it out together as fairly and equitably as possible. Don't assume that things will somehow just take care of themselves; that expectation often hides the assumption that things will work themselves out to your personal advantage. Be prepared to compromise, but not to sacrifice your needs or pressure your partner into something that feels wrong to him or her. Get counseling or have a friend help out the two of you if you hit upon a particularly thorny problem area that makes either of you too upset to continue talking calmly and respectfully. Finally, be open to change. Just because you're the chief provider or career climber in the earliest years of your relationship doesn't mean you'll always be. She may write that novel and turn out a bestseller that completely changes your life together.

Health

Particularly for older couples, physical health and vitality can be one of the major determinants of the mutual quality of life, yet not many people examine all aspects of the issue carefully. Two people in their fifties may have a dating relationship in which health issues never arise—but what if he has a chronic heart problem that will prevent him from going along on her strenuous mountain hikes? In general, we advise a full and open discussion of all health issues early in the process of deciding for commitment. It's fair for each partner to undergo complete physicals and share the results, so that no one is surprised by preexisting health conditions of a partner after mutual residence has been established or the marriage vows are taken.

WHAT KIND OF COMMITMENT? AND WHEN?

Although there is great variance in the speed at which couples develop intimacy and begin approaching the major issues of commitment, we offer a general rule of thumb that the discussion of these issues should begin somewhere between three and twelve months after a first date. Of course this assumes that a relationship is progressing relatively well and both people look forward to its deepening. Some people can be ready for commitment before three months, but for most that timing would probably be a little premature. If a couple has been together monogamously for most of a year and is not yet considering plans for the future, they run the risk of settling into an uncommitted limbo in which at least one partner is suffering frustration for the convenience of the other.

There's also the question of what kind of commitment is appropriate for a particular couple. People often ask us if we think living together before marriage is a good idea. Personally, John is a little more friendly to the idea than Julie is, but what matters is how the people actually involved feel about it—and whether they've really thought through the issues at hand. One thing's for sure: Moving in together just to save money on rent, without talking about the long-term future, is not the wisest course of action. Two questions that should be considered in deciding whether to marry or live together first include:

Do you see living together as a "dress rehearsal" for marriage, a substitute for marriage, or an avoidance of marriage? For some people, especially those who have become used to their single lifestyle over time, living together can be a useful rehearsal for a more permanent commitment. The romance of a dating relationship can undergo severe stress and strain when such people first try to merge their lifestyles on a daily basis, and some people may discover that they are better suited to loving and living apart than trying to live together the rest of their lives.

On the other hand, it's true that some people choose to live together because one or more of the partners likes the feeling of having an "easy out" if the going gets tough. These people fear the "for better or worse" kind of dedication implied by the marriage vows, and like the feeling of keeping their options open. But it shouldn't take very much discussion between two people to distinguish whether each of them looks at living together as preparation for the future or avoidance of real commitment. Tension, conflicts, and breakups are most likely to result when the issue hasn't been openly discussed and mutually decided—for example, when a woman who prefers marriage grudgingly goes along with a man who wants to live together first because that's "just how he feels" and gives her only a take-it-or-leave-it choice.

Finally, there are those couples, relatively rare by our observation, who simply don't need to get married to solidify and maintain a lasting commitment. They usually feel fairly free of family, peer, and religious influences, and see no particular material advantages in marriage. Still, it seems to us that most such couples tend to go ahead and get married a few years down the line, long after they have demonstrated that they can make their relationship work. Often these people feel that their partnership lacks only the subtle, spiritual effect of certifying their union that marriage provides.

Are you getting married because you're reasonably certain you can make your relationship work, or because you want to force it to work? The idea of commitment that marriage implies can be misused. If you're frustrated by long-standing communication difficulties in a relationship, or know or suspect that your partner is being unfaithful, getting married can seem to be a way to settle such problems once and for all. If you're married, you *have* to work it out, right? Such reasoning has led to more divorces than successful marriages. No couple should expect marriage to make them more committed; marriage only certifies and celebrates the commitment that you bring to it. It neither solves problems nor makes them go away all by itself; as we said earlier, it's not a magic act.

That's why one should be cautious about marrying at the height of a whirlwind romantic affair, before any significant problems or differences of opinion have arisen in a relationship. We've known people who have been through two or three divorces to get married again on a whim partly because of the belief that a quick marriage will somehow inoculate them against the problems that haunted their previous relationships. Rarely have we seen that bet pay off. Chronic problems of relating have to be solved by reflection, honest self-examination, and hard work on improving one's communication skills.

We don't mean to imply that one can move toward marriage only with an attitude of absolute certainty. Marriage is necessarily a realm of the unknown, and while two people can and should tentatively plan for all the stages of life that they will experience together, they can be sure of relatively little that will actually happen to them. (And that's what makes it so interesting!) A measure of anxiety and ambivalence will accompany every decision for marriage. An engaged couple needn't feel ashamed of this; in fact, the more they can talk about it the better. The key is for them to determine whether they can accept some uncertainty as part of their affirmation of wanting to stay together—come what may—or whether they are trying to stave off a massive anxiety that's actually rooted in a failure to communicate openly and respectfully. Since we've been talking so much about the importance of good communication, we'd be remiss not to leave you with a few essential guidelines.

FOUR GUIDELINES FOR IMPROVING COMMUNICATION SKILLS

What follows is not specific advice on how to improve your person-to-person communication; that's beyond the scope of this book and is best learned either in "on the job" training or with the help of a skilled counselor. But our observation of many, many intimate relationships, both failed and successful, has convinced us that it's easier for people to improve their communication skills when they've adopted at least one or two of the following guidelines. These can best be seen as goals to strive for; that means that no one should feel guilty or inadequate at times when they can't be fulfilled.

Instead, look on them as signposts pointing the way toward an open, understanding, and lasting intimate relationship. It's never too early, by the way, to discuss these guidelines with someone you're getting to know. How he or she responds to these ideas may give you valuable information on the potential of the relationship.

1. *Avoid blaming each other for problems in your relationship.* Making a joint agreement just to *try* giving up blame is a tremendous step forward for any couple. We have seen countless relationships broken up because one partner blames the other completely for their serious difficulties, thus avoiding shared responsibility and a more realistic perception of how their problems developed.

Giving up blaming does not mean letting anyone off the hook for unkind or divisive behaviors. But it does mean seeing the problems of either partner as *shared problems* that require mutual learning to resolve.

For instance, let's take the example of a young, newly married couple in which the husband, Dale, is a TV football fanatic. The issue of his rowdy Sunday afternoons in front of the tube with his best buddies never came up while Dale and his wife Carol were dating. But now that they are spending their first autumn together, Carol has been shocked to learn that Dale's pals are used to showing up without warning on Sundays, and then drinking beer, whistling, shouting, and stomping their way through the afternoon. After grinning and bearing it for a couple of weeks, she gets in the habit of going shopping on these days, only to come home and find her husband napping upstairs and the living room a total mess.

After the third or fourth weekly occurrence, Carol is so upset that she angrily confronts Dale and they get into a blaming game. "Why do you have to make so much noise and mess?" Carol cries, and Dale counters, "Why do you have to get so upset about it?"

To move beyond this stage, Carol and Dale will need to respect that they each have a real problem—she doesn't like the noise and mess of Dale's TV football habit, and Dale is upset that it bothers her. If they keep blaming each other, they will continue to assume that the other one is doing something wrong that must be stopped. But if they accept that the football issue is a shared problem for which they share equal responsibility, then they will be on the way to finding a mutually satisfying solution. Perhaps Dale can agree to meet his buddies at a sports bar at least half the time during football season; perhaps Carol can arrange to meet her friends on the Sundays that Dale's friends come over.

We find that couples stuck in the blame game are also very uncreative when it comes to problem solving. That's because they're so often using their energy against each other, instead of combining their energy. To avoid this kind of struggle, use this simple (if not always easy) process: First, agree beforehand that when either one of you has a problem with the relationship, *you have a shared problem.* Second, agree to avoid blaming each other in order to *see your shared problem as a learning task* that can eventually be mastered.

2. *Allow for the venting of frustration, hostility, and other negative feelings without assuming that your relationship has gone bad.* Particularly in the first few years of a new marriage or living-together relationship, a lot of adjustments have to be

made in two individual's lifestyles in order to merge them. We've seen a lot of people, particularly women, fear that they are being mean, small, or unfaithful if they ever have feelings of frustration or hostility toward their partner during this process. They will hold back on expressing those feelings until they build up and boil over someday. Men are more likely to stuff their feelings or take them out on a punching bag or the running track, but that's not the best solution either.

People will sometimes withhold their negative feelings from each other because they confuse moral prescriptions about how to *behave* with how they should *feel*. For instance, momentarily feeling like you could kill your spouse doesn't make you a murderer. It's actually far better to say, "You know, I could kill you for clipping your fingernails at dinner!" than to punish yourself inwardly for having such a bizarre thought but never expressing your irritation out loud. It's crucially important to have enough "space" in your emotional relationship to let strong negative feelings be vented, explored together, and settled down.

Couples sometimes reach a point where they are overwhelmed by a lot of long-suppressed angers and irritations, none of which would have been a big problem at the time. But when they must be dealt with all at once after ten or twenty years, they can be fatal to a relationship. Then people may end up in a matchmaker's office saying something like, "I don't know what went wrong with my marriage—suddenly it just seemed like nothing worked anymore." When we hear that kind of complaint, we know that we have a problematic prospect for a lasting match.

3. *Plan for regular "check-ins" to renew and refresh your in-*

timate communication. In these days of the two-career household, many couples simply get too busy to stay up-to-date on each others feelings and deepest concerns. Unless two people have the luxury of both working out of their home, they will probably need to plan regular getaways where they have ample time to review and talk over how their lives are going, both separately and together. In our experience, some of our most important decisions and turning points have been arrived at while away on vacations, and not always when we expected them to develop. Whenever possible, communication check-ins should not be squeezed into excursions that serve some other major purpose, like visiting in-laws or attending a business conference. If you have kids, you may want to consider arranging at least two or three short getaways yearly without them.

Some couples may also feel the need for more frequent check-ins on a home basis, monthly or perhaps even weekly. This can be necessary when your respective careers are so demanding that you actually see very little of each other from day to day, and cannot even share some of the shopping excursions and other household chores. If such a situation persists for too long, however, you may want to review whether this degree of dedication to your careers is healthy for both of you. We've known people who actually used their work to avoid chronic problems of relating at home, and that's a recipe for creating affairs, mutual resentment and suspicion, and a home life that consists of little more than "two ships passing in the night."

Finally, people who are reasonably comfortable with professional counseling may find it helpful to do some of their periodic check-ins with a relationship therapist, whether or not a big problem is on their minds at the time.

A caring professional who has insight into many different kinds of relationship situations may help you become aware of important issues that are developing beneath the surface of your everyday lives. Marriage counseling is becoming less and less stigmatized as a "rescue mission" these days, and there is an increasing variety of workshops and seminars available for couples who want to explore new approaches to emotional and sexual intimacy without feeling that there is anything "wrong" with them. If you see your relationship as a mutual learning venture, then it's easier to accept the advice and wisdom of outsiders as a helpful kind of teaching—rather than some kind of distasteful medicine.

4. *Aim for a mutual purpose that's bigger than just the two of you.* What we mean by this is making the decision to see your relationship as a potential service to others—whether they be your own children, the people you serve through your respective careers, or other couples who can learn from the way you communicate with each other. Your service may be an organized form of teamwork, like we have in J. Wingo International, or it may be less formal, like doing volunteer work together. Or it may be as subtle as the two of you counseling troubled friends. Whatever the form, the intent to serve more than your own needs is what counts.

What does altruism have to do with improving your communication? One benefit of serving others through your relationship is that it helps you keep both of you connected to the world around you, thus taking some of the focus off your own relationship when you may be too absorbed in your mutual problems or your immediate practical concerns. We've observed that the amount and severity of communication problems that two people have with each other are directly proportional to each person's selfishness.

That remains true after a couple has committed to a life to-gether. If they are considerate of each other but stingy with what they offer everyone else, their relationship will either be in serious trouble before long or simply be much less profound and enjoyable than it could be otherwise.

We think this is a particularly important point in these times when too many people have developed an ac-quisitive, suspicious, or desperate attitude about finding a romantic partner. Sensing that time is running out or wor-rying that they will somehow be cheated in the search for love, people can become predatory and self-serving while dating. If they somehow match up with someone despite these negative attitudes, they may then focus on getting everything they think they deserve as a couple—only to find themselves miserable after they've procured their house, put their children in the finest schools, and achieved success in their respective careers. Something will be miss-ing in their lives, and they won't know what it is.

To build a relationship that actually serves others is to achieve an authentic spiritual purpose in your life together, no matter what your religious beliefs or practice may be.

PREPARING FOR THE STAGES OF LIFE TOGETHER

In the most practical sense, there's no way you can prepare for all the stages of life you will go through to-gether as a committed couple. You can plan your children, but you can't know ahead of time who they will be as indi-viduals. You can try to plan your careers, but indications are that everyone's professional lives will continue to get more unpredictable as we approach the end of the century. And, most of all, you may start out your life with one kind of relationship but find that you develop and live through several different kinds of relationships as the years go by.

We've lived through different careers and resided in various parts of the country, raised two children (now young women), experienced severe monetary problems and satisfying financial success, and even weathered a brief separation in the last ten years. We couldn't have known ahead of time that all these things would happen exactly as they did. But we prepared for them the only way we knew how: by our shared commitment to the institution of marriage, and by our dedication to treating each other with respect, caring, and openness.

The most important preparation you can make for the stages of life together is a daily, mutual dedication to each other's happiness. This means checking in frequently on each other's feelings, hopes, and dreams. It means resisting the urge to blame each other for problems that arise, always trying to opt instead to see problems as learning challenges that you're both on the way to mastering. Finally, it means never assuming that you know all there is to know about your life partner—because the fact is that he or she is a wonder and a mystery that will never stop unfolding before you, if you're willing to pay attention.

We seek love relationships because we want certain things, but *what love has to offer us is infinitely more than what we want.* What some call "the grace of God" is the miraculous recognition of how lucky we are to be alive, to be in love, or even just to be looking for love. That's why we try constantly to remind our clients of all the opportunities they have to meet someone special and build a life in partnership. Again and again, we see that most people's difficulties in finding a partner arise from their own fixed ideas about what's possible and what isn't possible. So we try gently to remind everyone that only an open mind can let in luck, love, and grace. If reading this book has enabled you to open your mind just a little bit more than before, then we've done our job well enough. We congratulate you on the love that's surely coming your way.

Appendix

Special Messages
for Women and for Men

People sometimes ask one of us—either man-to-man or woman-to-woman—if there are any secrets or tips about dating members of the opposite sex. Apparently these folks expect us to have "insider information" that the other gender isn't privy to, or to know strategies, maneuvers, or tricks that will "drive women wild" or make a man say, "I do."

The bad news is that we have no such information, and we'd advise you to be wary of anyone who says they do. The good news is that you don't need any secrets or tips to succeed in your search for a lifelong mate, even in today's difficult social scene. You do need a good idea of who you are, a reflective and sensible grasp of what you desire in a mate, and an enthusiastic sense of what you have to offer someone. We hope this book has helped you develop more self-awareness in these respects than you had before reading it—because that's what counts in these days when so many people are busy being anyone but themselves.

Still, we thought it might be fun to write two final messages to our readers, one for women written by Julie and one for men written by John. We worked on these separately and they weren't revised to agree with each other afterward. While not summing up everything we've said so far, these messages offer a few of the most important points of advice that occurred to each of us while wrapping up the manuscript. This is what each of us might tell a client at the end of an interview, before arranging his or her first date with a prospect from the files of J. Wingo International. These messages are our send-off to you, too, and they come with our best wishes for finding the passion, intimacy, and mutual respect that you deserve in a lasting love.

A SPECIAL MESSAGE FOR WOMEN FROM JULIE

Although it may not always be this way, we women are still generally in the position of being pursued by men in the quest for a mate. Even if we actively take it upon ourselves to ask men out, we will find that cultural training and social influences still discourage us from being quite as assertive or aggressive as men while dating. Like it or not, then, our social role in the mating game has more to do with *availability* than *pursuit*. Yet because so many women have been disappointed or heartbroken in their relationship experiences, they increasingly tend to mask their availability to men as a means of self-defense. If you're neither pursuing men nor appearing very available to them, guess what?

Of course, it's important to present yourself, both physically and psychologically, with tact and taste. As I see them, these are some of the most important points for women who are trying to maintain the delicate balance between reasonable self-protection and availability for intimacy:

Don't tell too much too soon. I often hear that women tell too much of a personal nature too soon in an evolving relationship. We want to tell a man about ourselves and our past as a way of seeing how he reacts, hoping of course that he will be inspired to share the same kind of intimate information with us. This is fine, but care should be taken not to push it too far too quickly. You don't want it to appear as if there's nothing left to learn about you after two dates, or to be seen as unhealthy or still grieving over a lost relationship.

Never forget that the purpose of dating is to develop a sense of coming close to each other—emotionally, intellectually, and finally, physically. I believe that the healthiest bonding occurs slowly but progressively, not by "love at first sight." Even if you feel that way, don't let everything about you spill out at once. Let a series of dates give both of you the opportunity to give and receive bits of intimacy that gradually build the foundation of a strong, unfolding relationship.

Take responsibility for yourself. Avoid the temptation to blame our culture, your ex, or men in general for any lack of success in finding a partner. For example: Men almost always overstress a woman's physical attractiveness in their search for a mate. Rather than curse that reality, try to use it to your advantage. Joining a fitness club to improve your physique can also make you healthier over the long term; the same goes for losing extra weight. If you're fixated on the idea that a man must like you just the way you are, regardless of how unhealthy or unattractive you may be, then

217

you may be feeling righteous by yourself for a long time to come.

If you're a busy career woman, be careful not to blame your work situation for limiting your access to men. You can always network with friends and associates, try personal ads, or see a matchmaker. Evaluate what's socially limiting in your everyday environment, and do something definite to alter it.

Make sure you're not developing a "hard shell." This is the most frequent problem I see with our women clients who are past their twenties—an impassive facial mask and behavior that's seemingly gender-neutral. But men still need and value softness and femininity, and you can show that you have those qualities without making yourself look like a potential victim. To effectively cover your femininity as a way of avoiding subsequent relationship failure does ensure that you won't feel that pain again. It may also ensure that you will confuse men and drive them away.

You can state your mind and your conditions for respectful relating without becoming hard and cold. It's true that you may be rejected or lied to, but you can use your past bitter experiences to become wiser, more alert, and more compassionate about the failures of men. After all, they're only human like you. Just don't give up. Your lifelong mate is somewhere out there for you, if you approach him thoughtfully, actively, and tactfully.

A SPECIAL MESSAGE FOR MEN FROM JOHN

Men, the "rules" for dating have changed dramatically in the '90s. The less time you spend complaining and the more effort you make to embrace the changes that the times demand of us, the higher your chances of finding a lifelong mate. The following five points are derived from my years as a professional matchmaker as well as my experience in academia and the corporate world. I like to think of myself as pragmatic, and these are my no-nonsense guidelines for men who are looking for love:

Never forget that every man has a mate waiting somewhere for him. The pool of potentially compatible females is large as long as your requirements are not rigidly unrealistic or clearly out of whack with what you have to offer a woman. Stop looking for the perfect partner—she doesn't exist. Shoot for 80 percent of what you want, and keep at it.

Don't overemphasize visual beauty in your screening of potential partners. The simple fact is that we men react more strongly to physical appearance than women do, but we must remember not to let that criterion overrule all others. Think hard about what else has attracted you to women you've loved or strongly liked—a mischievous twinkle in her eye? A challenging intellect? An easy laugh? A maternal or sensual air? You might find it helpful to make a list of the nonphysical attributes that you find attractive, especially if you're chronically attracted to certain physical "types" of women who are otherwise all wrong for you.

I strongly believe that a woman of average physical beauty with the right mix of appealing character traits will make a better partner than a "nine" or "ten" beauty with whom you can't hold a conversation. Remember that you're seeking a mate for life—not a date for the prom or a trophy that will impress other men.

Avoid being pushy about sex early in a relationship. Most women have been pressured by men about sex for their entire adult lives. Therefore most women place a very high value on the man who respects sexual intimacy for what it should be: a special interaction that grows out of mutual trust, respect, and love. The man who demands premature intimacy is giving the message that his need for sex overrules the woman's feelings. That's not the route to a long-term love.

Remember that women ask for integrity in a man more than any other trait. They want men to be who they say they are, to be truthful about their relationship situation, and not to lie about their intents or feelings in order to get close physically. Never try deliberately to impress a woman—it's very likely to backfire and make her distrust you. Women are generally more intuitive than we are, and they can sense when a man is confident enough in himself not to have to pretend to be something he isn't. Be tactful, but let her know the real you from the start. If she's the right one for you, you may be surprised to learn that she's already figured it out and is simply waiting for you to confirm her perceptions.

Take stock of what you have to offer her and compare it to your wish list for a mate. I've seen many men looking for fantasy fulfillment when they'd be better off making a pragmatic list of what they'd like to find in a woman, especially in light of their own pros and cons. Face the facts: If you're average-looking, your mate will probably be average-looking too. Don't lead yourself on. It only leads to frustration and a predictable lack of success.

In sum, I advise men to take stock of themselves, be honest about who they are, be realistic about what they want, and attend to *her* needs and feelings first. Above all, don't give up. Pay attention to these touchstones and you will be on your way to a great romance and a solid relationship.